Politics in Action

Cases in Modern
American Government

Politics in Action

Cases in Modern American Government

Gary Wasserman
The Johns Hopkins University–Nanjing Center

Houghton Mifflin Company
Boston New York

Publisher: Charles Hartford
Sponsoring Editor: Katherine Meisenheimer
Assistant Editor: Christina Lembo
Editorial Assistant: Kristen Craib
Senior Project Editor: Kerry Doyle
Executive Marketing Manager: Nicola Poser
Marketing Associate: Kathleen Mellon

Cover image: © Jim Wehtje/Photodisc Green at GettyImages.com

Printed in the U.S.A.

Library of Congress Control Number: 2005924906

ISBN: 0-618-47416-1

3456789-MP-09 08 07 06

To my family

Contents

chapter 12   THE BUREAUCRACY

The *Columbia* and *Challenger* Disasters   143
Groupthink in a Bureaucracy

chapter 13   THE JUDICIARY

Watergate, *U.S. v. Nixon*, and the U.S. Supreme Court   156

Preface

Like many political scientists, I got into the discipline because I thought politics was exciting and important. After working for a number of years in Washington, I returned to teaching hoping to communicate the excitement and importance of American politics to college students. There were frustrations.

My students, with some exceptions, didn't feel the same interest in the subject as their teacher. There were many reasons for this indifference, beyond the quality of the instruction. But that still left me with the task of involving students in the study of issues that I found fascinating. I wanted them to be familiar with the contemporary history that formed the context and language of our class discussions. Moreover, I needed to do it in a way that could compete with the distractions of modern media that were more entertaining to them than readings in American government.

The thirteen cases that follow are a step in re-engaging students. They present brief histories of important events in modern American politics and tie these events to the chapters of an introductory course. As snapshots of America's politicians and reporters, parties and bureaucracies, judges and lobbyists, the cases allow teachers to extend textbook concepts. In short, these are stories of how the game of American politics is played.

Goals of the Text

Some of these stories reflect original research, such as the case of pension reform in Congress (Chapter 10); some are adapted from the work of others, such as the shuttle disasters (Chapter 12); and still others reflect material that I've used in class over the years, such as the campaign for health care reform (Chapter 8). They have three objectives.

The first is to show contemporary politics in action. The cases present students with a revealing look at our country's political institutions and actors. We see

President George W. Bush using his public status to protect bureaucrats after 9/11 for their intelligence lapses, even as he depends on them for the coming invasion of Afghanistan; we hear a young campaign manager explain how his congressman plays the "redistricting racket" to ensure reelection; we go on campus to debate the current clash on the boundaries between free speech and harassment; and we look over the shoulders of the founding fathers as they sit down to dinner to reach a secret bargain to relocate the nation's capital.

The cases are organized to parallel the chapters in an introductory American government textbook, from the framers of the Constitution to civil liberties, from public opinion to media, from Congress to the judiciary. Yet the political actors in these cases cannot be contained in one chapter in a text, any more than they can be confined in real life. Their multiple appearances enrich these stories for teaching. For example, media appears in its designated chapter on the Lewinsky scandal (Chapter 9). But media puts in an appearance in other chapters as well: It figures into the campaign for health care reform (Chapter 8), into the president's response to 9/11 (Chapter 11), and in uncovering the Watergate scandal (Chapter 13). Even media's absence has something to teach. Its minor role in Congress's consideration of pension reform (Chapter 10) speaks volumes about the numerous major public policy issues that are ignored by the press.

The second goal is to illustrate political science concepts. The concepts focus our thinking about the behavior of the government institutions and political actors under scrutiny. The concepts help explain the cases. While most chapters have one major focus—groupthink in the bureaucracy chapter on the shuttle disasters (Chapter 12), or the idea of "going public" in examining interest groups' responses to a president's proposal for health care reform (Chapter 8), many of these cases spill over conceptual confines to teach other lessons as well. One brief chapter on abortion (Chapter 5) touches on the social revolution of the sixties, the impact of the women's movement, the effort of pro and anti abortion groups to frame the issue, the two-way influence of government leaders and public opinion, the issue of partial-birth abortion, the role of the Supreme Court in policymaking, and the rationality of popular opinion. Other chapters contain similarly overlapping themes that can be uncovered in class discussions.

The third goal of this text is to make students familiar with American political history. Materials used in introductory classes often premise a background that many students don't have. Assuming that most know about the events surrounding Clinton's impeachment or Watergate or even the 9/11 terrorist attacks is a mistake only discovered too late in a course. Modern history is the laboratory where political scientists make their observations, conduct their experiments, and collect data. Students need to be familiar with it. Aspects of these historical events have entered into the language of politics with terms such as downsizing, fighting words, speech codes, unfunded mandates, voter targeting, leaks, grassroots tactics, sound bites, and feeding frenzy. Students may know something about these references; they seldom know enough. Shown in their real world settings, the cases illustrate the origins and uses of these textbook phrases.

Organization

Divided into three sections, the thirteen case stories follow the order of an introductory American government text. The first section covers the foundations of American politics: the constitutional period, federalism, civil rights, and civil liberties. Next is the public, the groups and structures that link citizens with the policy process: public opinion, campaigns and elections, political parties, interest groups, and media. The final section includes the institutions of the national government: Congress, the presidency, the bureaucracy, and the judiciary. The cases extend the historical and functional discussion of a textbook by examining the actual political behavior of these institutions and groups.

In addition, there are several organizational aids for students. An introduction at the beginning of each chapter briefly establishes a connection to the concepts discussed in class and frames the issues presented in the case study. A "Concepts Highlighted" feature directly following the case introduction helps students read for the key concepts presented in the case.

Instructor Resources

An Instructor's Resource Manual with Test Items accompanies this text. It contains a Topical Table of Contents outlining which cases illustrate which topics, plus Teaching Notes, multiple-choice questions, and essay questions for each of the thirteen cases.

Acknowledgments

This is a collection written by the author but dependent on the work of many others. The first group includes the many scholars cited in the footnotes and on whose original works most of these cases rest. I hope this volume pays adequate tribute to them and motivates the reader to delve deeper into the subjects by consulting their fuller treatment. For their comments on earlier drafts, I'd like to thank Professors Kenneth R. Bowling, Melvin J. Dubnick, Bob Lieber, Ed Wasserman, and Clyde Wilcox. Others who provided valuable comments on the chapters include Abi Awomolo, Clark Atlanta University; Mark Brewer, Colby College; Carl D. Cavalli, North Georgia College and State University; Steven Greene, North Carolina State University; Jim Hutter, Iowa State University; Mehnaaz Momen, Texas

A&M International University; Francis Moran, New Jersey City University; David Paul, The Ohio State University at Newark; and George E. Shambaugh, Georgetown University. I would also like to thank the following teachers of college-level preparatory courses for offering comments on the manuscript: Daron F. Absher, Carbondale Community High School (Carbondale, IL); Ann H. Connor, Academy of Notre Dame (Villanova, PA); Van Hadley, Roy High School (Roy, UT); D. Keith McBrayer, Denison High School (Denison, TX); and Karen Waples, Cherry Creek High School (Englewood, CO).

I started this book while teaching at Georgetown University and finished it as a visiting professor at Johns Hopkins' School of Advanced International Studies, Nanjing Center, China. I'd like to thank both universities.

Nadia Khawaja provided excellent research and insights. Chris Castleberry helped start the process as my teaching assistant at Georgetown University. My colleagues, including Professor Jim Riedel of The Johns Hopkins University, Nanjing Center, and Jim Smith and Greg Andrews at Smith, Dawson and Andrews, one of Washington's leading lobbying firms, were supportive throughout the process. Others who helped include my family, notably son Daniel, daughter Laura, and wife Ann, all of whom grounded me in the thinking of readers.

The people of Houghton Mifflin were enthusiastic, informative, and, when needed, supportive. Oscar Shepherd first encouraged me to look to his publisher. Katherine Meisenheimer saw the book through from the beginning, and Christina Lembo was a clear-eyed editor as the manuscript turned into a book. Others working behind the scenes included Kerry Doyle and Nancy Benjamin.

The mistakes are despite this help and are mine.

Gary Wasserman
Nanjing, China

Politics
in Action

Cases in Modern
American Government

chapter 1

The Meal Deal

The Dinner Table Bargain of 1790

Many Americans picture the founding fathers as a heavenly choir, harmonizing a constitutional hymn to the republic. Not quite. While both the breadth of their vision and the height of their accomplishments deserve our respect, a closer look reveals politicians going about the messy uncertainties of creating a nation.

These men are not diminished by being called politicians. They were practical men who were not about to loosen their grip on the daily tasks of governing, or pursuing their own interests, in a period of great change. Throughout the early years of the republic, these leaders had to both represent their regions and compromise to shape a lasting Union.

The story that follows embodies some of the conflicts, compromises, and personalities of the period immediately following the adoption of the U.S. Constitution. It tells the story of what a historian called "one of the most complex, fascinating, and controversial political deals in American history."[1] The Compromise of 1790 established the site of the nation's capital on the banks of the Potomac River while securing the financial stability of the new government. It was a trade done on behalf of conflicting regional and economic interests. Both sides gained, and the infant republic survived. So if we don't find angels singing on cue, then the drumbeat of a politician's victory march will have to do.

Much of what follows came from a dinner at Thomas Jefferson's house. Dining with him on that warm June night in 1790 were Alexander Hamilton and James Madison.

My thanks to Professor Kenneth R. Bowling, Professor George W. Carey, and Ellen Clark for their comments on this chapter.

concepts highlighted

1. The **north-south regional conflict** looms over this bargain. Are there hints of irreconcilable differences between the regions that would later surface in a civil war? Was this a reasonable compromise, or was Jefferson correct in saying that his side had lost?

2. Often their **states' interests predominated** in these men's calculations. To what extent were the key figures representing their states' narrow interests, and to what extent were they speaking for their own conflicting visions for the new republic?

3. **International weakness and domestic turmoil** loomed as great threats to all the founders, encouraging them toward compromise. Which side in this conflict seems most threatened by the prospect of the Union dissolving? Is Hamilton a "nationalist," while Jefferson is for states' rights?

4. Much of what the framers accomplished could be described as **a marriage of interest and principle**. President Washington's lobbying to locate the capital near his lands on the Potomac River reveals the blend of ideals and self-interest that motivated him. At that time, did this reflect a conflict of interest between Washington's public role and his private wealth? Would it be seen differently today? Are all the parties violating their democratic principles by not having the compromise publicly debated?

According to Thomas Jefferson, he got involved in the issue through a chance encounter: He bumped into Alexander Hamilton on the street. Actually, Jefferson was waiting outside George Washington's presidential office on Broadway in New York City, where in June 1790 the Constitution's first administration was based. The two did not know each other well, even though Jefferson was secretary of state and Hamilton was secretary of the treasury.

Neither was in the best of spirits. Jefferson was just recovering from one of his frequent migraine headaches, this one lasting over a month. Hamilton, who was usually well dressed and confident, appeared disheveled and depressed. Jefferson described him as a beaten man—"somber, haggard, and dejected beyond comparison." Hamilton declared he was prepared to resign from the cabinet and feared the Union was coming apart.

What had upset Hamilton was the stalemate in Congress over whether the new government would take responsibility for state debts. This was a key part of Hamilton's grand plan to firmly establish the public credit of the United States as a reliable borrower among the nations of the world. It was being blocked by a group of southern congressmen led by James Madison, Jefferson's friend and protégé. Jefferson, who claimed ignorance of the matter—having recently returned from his post as U.S. minister in Paris—offered to host a dinner at his house for the two rivals. It would be a private affair, where, over wine and good food, the three of them could have, in Jefferson's words, "a friendly discussion of the subject."

In writing his account of the evening two years later, Jefferson soft-pedaled what one historian called "the most meaningful dinner party in American history."[2] Probably held on Sunday, June 20, the meal deal would pave the way for Hamilton's centralizing financial plan and establish the seat of government (only to be more grandly referred to as "the nation's capital" in the mid-nineteenth century) that was sandwiched between two southern states. Jefferson brokered a political bargain that would mediate differences between state and national loyalties, between agrarian and urban interests, and between those wanting a feeble government and those wanting a strong one. The simmering North-South conflict would be deferred that night, only to surface again for resolution in future compromises and a later generation's civil war.

Guess Who's Coming to Dinner

Accounts of the day give a clear picture of the diners. Hamilton, thirty-five years old at the time, was an administrative and financial genius—bold, disciplined, and confident, and determined to establish a strong central government supported by a ruling class based on industry and finance. He had the energy of his decisive convictions and a bulldog tendency to charge straight at an issue. In contrast to Jefferson's blue blood and inherited estate, Hamilton had been born in the West Indies, the illegitimate son in a broken home of an unsuccessful Scottish businessman and an independent-minded, frequently disgraced French woman. He had come to America poor. A compact figure at 5 feet 6 inches, with a crisp military bearing, he had risen to a position of equality among the wealthy, urban commercial classes he ably represented.[3]

Madison was Hamilton's age but even shorter, described as "no bigger than half a piece of soap." He was frail in appearance, easily mistaken for a shy librarian. But his gentle manner was deceptive. It concealed a stealth that disarmed opponents with the simple brilliance of his thoughts. In the two years since he had collaborated with Hamilton on the *The Federalist* papers, his nationalist loyalties had returned home to Virginia, which elected him to Congress. He now opposed Hamilton, speaking for the interests of his state's planter class, who feared a central government that would threaten their power, their rights, and their slaves.

Madison was Jefferson's loyal lieutenant, the detail man—a collaboration being renewed after Jefferson's five years in France. At forty-seven Jefferson was older than both Hamilton and Madison and, standing 6 feet 2 inches, reinforced his position as the senior member at dinner. He could not stand

Washington's first cabinet. From left to right: President Washington, Secretary of War Henry Knox, Secretary of the Treasury Alexander Hamilton (standing), Secretary of State Thomas Jefferson, and Attorney General Edmund Randolph.
Currier and Ives print, 1876, © Corbis

personal conflict and had been glad to miss the rough politics surrounding the adoption of the Constitution. He seemed happier reading the classics, usually in Greek and Latin, and avoided public debates. At the time of the dinner Jefferson was not widely known to have penned the Declaration of Independence. With untidy clothes and rambling sentences he looked the part of an absentminded professor.

The contrast with his rival Hamilton was unmistakable. Jefferson was the idealistic dreamer, an aristocrat who was ever hopeful of democracy's potential. Hamilton was a pessimist about human nature, putting his faith in a structured social order ruled by an elite of merit and money. Hamilton radiated intensity; Jefferson had a laidback carelessness about him. Hamilton spoke for six hours in his initial "remarks" to the Constitutional Convention. John Adams reported that he couldn't recall Jefferson uttering more than two or three sentences, even in committee, when he was in the Continental Congress. On a personal level, "women found [Hamilton] irresistible, but they did not care much for Jefferson."[4]

Jefferson was a lukewarm supporter of the Constitution and had only reluctantly returned from Europe to join Washington's administration and the

A young James Madison, described at the time as "no bigger than half a piece of soap."
Painting by Charles Peale (1741–1827), photo by MPI/Getty Images

political infighting that both his guests had perfected. But Jefferson was well aware of the present danger challenging the fragile republic. In a letter to another future president, James Monroe, Jefferson wrote that he felt a compromise on debt payment was necessary "for the sake of union, and to save us from the greatest of all calamities, the total extinction of our credit in Europe." Jefferson warned, "If this plan of compromise does not take place, I fear one infinitely worse."[5] Indeed, what had led up to the dinner made his worries seem well-founded.

Background to the Compromise

The issue of paying off state debts, called assumption, was tying up Congress in knots. It had overwhelmed all other debates, including where to locate the new nation's capital. Hamilton asked Congress in January 1790 to refund at face value all the paper money and certificates that had been used to pay soldiers and suppliers during the Revolutionary War. For Hamilton, assuming the war debt of the states with new federal bonds paying interest was a blessing in disguise. It would cement the union, revitalize the country's lagging economic growth, tie wealthy creditors' interests to the success of the Union, and enable the new republic to take its place in the ranks of nations honoring their war debts.

What seemed eminently fair on the surface, however, launched bitter opposition. Many soldiers who had been paid in seemingly worthless currency had over the years sold this paper to speculators at considerably less than face value. Now it would not be the veterans who profited from their military service but the speculators. Also, raising the fury of opponents were the stories that associates of Hamilton had been leaked details of his plan before they were released to the public. They and congressmen from New England and New York promptly sent agents into the countryside, notably North Carolina, to buy up notes from the unknowing. At a quarter on the dollar it was a dream scam for political insiders.[6]

Like most of the major controversies of these early years, this conflict rumbled along regional fault lines. Massachusetts held a large part of the debt, while Virginia's remaining debt was small. As the most populous state, Virginia would pay the heaviest taxes to fund this new national debt while already having paid off much of its own. Virginia led the fight against assumption, which quickly took on a North-South dimension—even though South Carolina held the largest per capita debt and opposed assumption. With one-fifth the nation's population, one-third its commerce, and an elite that felt it had practically won the war alone, Virginia (where "all Geese are Swans," declared John Adams) was not about to surrender to a central government run by northern financiers.

Southern representatives defeated Hamilton's proposal for assumption in the House. Madison's counterproposal to discriminate between original and present holders of the securities was dismissed by Hamilton as naive and unrealistic. (How could these multiple transactions ever be sorted out?) Hamilton responded that there would be no repayment of loans to Holland and France, whose money had been critical to winning the war. The new government could not pay its overseas creditors—or New York speculators for that matter. The stalemate over assumption caused Congress to grind to a halt. Would the Union survive?[7]

Finding the Way to the Capital

The fight over locating the new nation's capital had been simmering for as long as the debt issue. This generation of leaders had fought over the locations of county seats and state capitals, and they knew the practical benefits associated with capital cities. Property values near these sites would skyrocket, thus enriching large landowners. Access to government offices benefited the well placed in the form of legislation, contracts, and jobs. The entire local economy would get a boost from a government providing improved transportation and military protection.[8]

Questions of regional influence were never far below the surface. Power and prestige would come to the region closest to the capital. The great North-South division loomed over the issue. The South, already sensitive to being a minority within the Union, felt it needed leverage to be heard in national forums on the divisive issue of slavery. The West, too, where the country's future expansion lay, wanted a voice in the decision. On the positive side, a capital properly located could knit together the competing regions and ensure the survival of the Union. The geography underlying this goal narrowed the possibilities to locations accessible to both the West and the Atlantic Ocean and near the country's center.

Alas, definitions of "center" varied. The North argued that it should be based on population and found that to be close to Philadelphia. The South made the point that territory was more important, insisting that the future westward growth of the Union should be taken into account. The South's argument was further bolstered by the knowledge that the geographic midpoint between the northern and southern boundaries of the United States (northern Maine and southern Georgia) was on the Potomac River, near Georgetown. And with spiritual overtones, the spot pointed to was literally next door to the home of the nation's leading citizen, the first president of the United States and owner of Mount Vernon, Virginia.

By 1790 the political debate over the site of the new capital had narrowed. The great mid-coastal rivers and the cities on them competed to become the main avenue for economic development of the expanding American empire. In these pre-railroad years, major rivers were the interstate highways to the wealth of the interior—the Hudson ending in New York City's harbor, the Delaware River championed by Philadelphia, the Susquehanna emptying into Chesapeake Bay above Baltimore, or the Potomac linked to the Ohio River and promoted by Virginians. Although each side made the case in terms of the benefits to the new Union, all pushed their own interests. As one observer said at the time, "It . . . amuses me to see the arguments our grave politicians bring forward when I know it will be determined by local Interests."[9] The debate swirled among interests representing three cities: New York, where in 1790 Congress was meeting; Philadelphia, the traditional home of Congress during the Revolution; and the not-yet-built city on the Potomac.

Working behind the scenes to powerfully promote the Potomac location was George Washington. He envisioned the metropolis of America on the banks of the river, enriching his nation, his state, and himself.[10] A landowner and explorer of the region, Washington had long sought navigation improvements to the Potomac based on the misconception that it offered a direct link between the American interior and Chesapeake Bay. On leaving command of the army in 1783, he declared that only one public project interested him: opening up the Potomac above Georgetown. He became president of the Potomac Company, which aimed to do exactly that. As a young man Washington had fallen victim to "Potomac Fever" and held on to this lifelong obsession for making the river the gateway to the future wealth of the West.

In Washington's era, political leaders saw little conflict between their public goals and their private interests. Mount Vernon's ten miles of Potomac River frontage, next to the federal district he selected, was only the beginning of Washington's lands. Of the other 60,000 acres he owned throughout the country, some two-thirds of it was along the Potomac-Ohio river system, which would benefit from improved navigation. When he asked Congress to expand the federal district to Alexandria—risking the greatest public criticism of his presidency—it meant including 1,200 acres of woodland he owned as well as his wife's family's 950-acre plantation that would later become Arlington National Cemetery.[11] Nor was the increased land wealth in the new capital a small matter. John Adams somewhat sourly thought Washington's choice of a capital had raised the value of his properties by 1,000 percent. Adams wasn't far off the mark. In October 1791, after the district had been selected, the price for a lot averaged around $265. A few years earlier, a good price for one acre containing eleven lots was $50—when you could sell them at all.[12]

Washington's motives were not only land speculation. Creating a federal city that would be the equal to any in Europe was a "key component" of his nationalist vision.[13] While masking his own role, he had worked with Jefferson and Madison for seven years to place the capital on the Potomac. Now the moment had arrived.

The Compromise of 1790

The two great questions of funding the debt and fixing the seat of government have been agitated, as was natural, with a good deal of warmth as well as ability. . . . They were more in danger of having convulsed the government Itself than any other points.

George Washington, August 10, 1790

The bargaining surrounding the compromise was a complex chess game. It involved a three-dimensional conflict of regional, economic, and national interests. The states alone represented a wide variety of concerns—wider than found in modern politics. An elected official from Virginia or Pennsylvania might be representing interests that today would speak through lobbyists, trade associations, political parties, media, and government agencies. This less specialized political system directly channeled the economic, political, and regional forces through a small number of leaders. This meant that a leader like Jefferson could be speaking for slaveholding plantations, rural debtors, small farmers, the state of Virginia, the entire southern region, or his own populist ideology.

The meal deal cut by Jefferson, Hamilton, and Madison during their June 20 gathering had several moving parts. One element was to locate the capital in Philadelphia for ten years. The Pennsylvanians thought that getting the temporary capital out of New York would be good enough, somewhat smugly concluding that no city would ever be built on the Potomac that could lure Congress away from the bright lights of Philadelphia. Their brief alliance with the Virginians was based on this misunderstanding.

While the friends of New York wanted Congress to stay next to Wall Street, there was something more dear to them than location. Many New Yorkers had a direct financial interest in the repayment of state debts, which they were owed. The Virginians, who were blocking assumption, were in a position to help. At the Jefferson dinner Madison agreed that although he could not himself vote for the bitterly opposed assumption, he would stop organizing against it and "leave it to its fate." This was provided, of course, that Hamilton could offer assistance on that other issue of moving the capital. Jefferson put it this way.

> It was observed, I forget by which one of them, that as the pill would be a bitter one to Southern States, something should be done to soothe them, that the removal of the seat of Government to the Patowmac was a just measure, & would probably be a popular one with them and would be a proper one to follow assumption.[14]

Implementing the Bargain

Carrying out the compromise involved the sort of wheeling and dealing familiar to modern students of Congress. Madison secured votes for assumption from four congressmen whose districts either bordered on or had an interest in the Potomac. One was assured that if Georgetown was given the capital, his town of Alexandria would be included in the federal district. Two members of the Carroll family of Maryland who were serving in Congress signed on as supporters of assumption. Part of the price of their agreement was that all the public buildings in the capital would be restricted to the Maryland side of the Potomac. The Carroll family's holdings of tens of thousands of acres in the area of the future capital did not go unnoticed.

New England supporters of assumption kept their part of the bargain. They backed the core agreement for moving the temporary capital from New York to Philadelphia followed by the establishment of a permanent one on the Potomac. Hamilton cemented Virginia's agreement to assumption by reworking the numbers of its financial obligations. In the revised version, Virginia's assumed debt and its federal taxes owed turned out "rather miraculously" to be the same: $3.5 million. Assumption became a wash for Virginia. Adding in the rewards from locating the new capital on its northern border (estimated by Jefferson at half a million a year), Virginia came out the clear financial winner.[15]

Soon after the dinner, the House passed the seat of government bill on July 9. By July 16, 1790, President Washington had signed it. Within days, the funding bill, including assumption, passed the House. On July 21 it passed the Senate by one vote. The link between the two issues was kept secret but was widely suspected.

Both sides of the bargain had public opponents. Southern newspapers carried letters that called for dissolving the Union rather than accepting assumption. In Virginia, under the leadership of anti-federalists like Patrick Henry, the legislature adopted a resolution denouncing assumption as "fatal to the existence of American liberty." Hamilton, smelling the threat of secession, warned that this was "the first symptom of a spirit which must either be killed or will kill the constitution of the United States." Moving the capital in exchange for assumption was called a bribe by a New York editor "to the lasting disgrace of the majority in both houses." The first cartoon attacking a president of the United States accused Washington of signing the seat of government bill for "self-gratification." New England journals ridiculed placing the seat of empire on a creek on the "wild and savage" Potomac. Most in Congress doubted they would ever relocate to a "wigwam place" more suited for hunters and hermits.[16]

Like political deals, then and now, the focus now moved to whether it could be carried out. Washington's strategy, pursued by Jefferson and Madison, was to prevent the issue of the capital's location from ever coming before Congress again. This meant appropriating once, in 1790, all the money that would be needed to move the capital. The decisions about the size, location, and shape of the new federal city would rest solely with the president. Congress had in its bill authorized Washington to place the capital anywhere along 110 miles of the Potomac. To avoid returning to Congress for money, Washington negotiated with landholders to donate land for the capital that the government could then sell to raise funds for construction. Landholders would exchange parcels of land with the understanding that their remaining holdings would appreciate handsomely. Before finalizing the location, Washington encouraged offers all along the river, shrewdly getting rival bids to keep land prices low for the government.

His decision to locate the capital to the east of Georgetown was announced in January 1791. By March, Washington had negotiated Congress's approval for adding his hometown of Alexandria to the federal district, a controversy that brought down rare public criticism on the president. Jefferson urged that construction begin as soon as possible. This savvy tactic (often used by modern bureaucrats) aimed to physically commit the government to its existing policy and to undermine Philadelphia's hopes of extending its hold on the seat of government. By the time Washington retired to Mount Vernon in 1797, the only opposition to the 1800 move to the Potomac existed in Philadelphia. A large majority of Americans favored it. To refuse such a move would, an English visitor wrote at the time, destroy the harmony of the Union, if not the Union itself.[17]

After Dinner

The three diners continued their distinguished careers, some with differing views of the evening's handiwork. Two years after the historic meal, Jefferson told Washington (for whom he may have been informally acting by holding the dinner) that the bargain was the greatest political mistake of his life. He believed Hamilton had "duped" him and that assumption had given eastern financial interests the power to control the government's finances. The location of the capital seemed of little importance by comparison. In terms of the Constitution, Jefferson saw, correctly as it turned out, that Congress's use of implied powers to enact Hamilton's plans paved the way for a federal government that would grow in power at the expense of the states.

The dinner marked a new flowering of Jefferson's collaboration with Madison. Their partnership propelled both to the presidency. Jefferson would assume that office because of the political groundwork, the party building, and the strategies carried out by Madison. Madison was Jefferson's Karl Rove (George W. Bush's powerful political advisor) and more, the chief operative who established the Republican-Democratic party and utterly destroyed the opposition Federalists. Madison's final act to save the 1790 Compromise came in 1814, when as president during the War of 1812 he fled the British burning of the Capitol and the White House. Afterward, pressure in Congress mounted for removing the capital from its precarious perch. Madison let it be known that he would veto such a measure. He reminded citizens of General Washington's commitment to the Potomac, and he labeled any move as a cowardly response to the English assault. When this crisis passed, the capital's site, despite several attempts to move it over the next half century, was largely secure.[18]

For Hamilton, assumption had been only one part of his plans for the nation's finances. As the nation's first secretary of the treasury, his goal was to fashion a unified government to stand as the equal of the great powers of Europe. To do this he proposed a program of taxes, mostly on trade, the encouragement of manufacturing, and the creation of a national bank. Establishing the credit of the United States was essential for gaining the confidence of foreign and domestic lenders and allowing the government to borrow in the future. Hamilton's economic vision would become the financial base for the growth of a powerful federal government. Understandably, Hamilton's statue stands alone today at the entrance of the U.S. Treasury Department.

Hamilton's plans for a strong government ran directly into Jefferson's dream of a decentralized agrarian republic. As political enemies, their arguments defined the first decade of the Constitution. Washington's support for Hamilton's program led to Jefferson leaving the cabinet in 1792. Despite the depth of their rivalry, it was ironically Hamilton's respect for Jefferson that eventually led to the younger man's death. When the presidential election of 1800 was thrown into the House of Representatives because both Jefferson and his running mate, Aaron Burr, got the same number of Electoral College votes—a constitutional oversight corrected by the Twelfth Amendment—it was up to the opposing Federalist party to decide who should be president. By strongly endorsing Jefferson as a man of character, Hamilton helped resolve the deadlock and gave Jefferson the presidency. This cemented Hamilton and Burr as implacable enemies, a bitterness that ended on the morning of July 11, 1804, with a duel between the two and the death of Alexander Hamilton.

Washington remained deeply attached to the "federal city" that was named after him in 1791. He devoted his energies to the details, including appointing the commissioners who would manage the district and personally resolving most of the crises that arose. He selected, worked with, and defended the young French-born planner P. Charles L'Enfant in mapping out the broad avenues and landscapes of the city. Political compromises were hardwired into the capital. The long distance between the White House and the Capitol building came from the need to reconcile competing groups of landowners by using land in each of their territories. Naming the central street that linked both branches of government "Pennsylvania Avenue" was a gesture meant to appease opponents in Philadelphia. Even locating the public buildings in the flat river plains of the Potomac rather than the hills above Georgetown reflected the General's bow to republican principles rather than monarchical heights. Jefferson's refusal to bury Washington in his capital had similar motives.[19]

Curiously, both Washington and Jefferson got the nation's capital wrong: Washington misstated its importance; Jefferson understated it.

Washington was the rare American leader of that time who had never been to Europe. This reflected his core belief that America's future lay in the other direction, to the west. Yet, he was wrong that the main route to this expanding American empire was through a navigable Potomac. By 1828 ground was broken for a railroad from Baltimore into the Ohio Valley to link the mid-Atlantic with the interior. The completion of the Erie Canal in New York three years earlier had connected the upper Midwest to the coast, elevating the port of

A view of Washington, DC, in 1810 illustrates the capital's modest beginnings. The President's House (not yet the more familiar White House) is in the upper right. Next to it is the Treasury Department and a local hotel.
This item is reproduced by permission of The Huntington Library, San Marino, California

New York and further dimming the attraction of the Potomac route. The economic vitality of Washington, DC, would have to wait for another century. And even then this prosperity would have little to do with access to the West and more to do with Hamilton's financial vision.

As the first president to serve his full term in the new capital, Jefferson helped realize his predecessor's dreams for the city. Yet, by viewing the Compromise of 1790 as a defeat, he seems to have understood the centralizing impact of Hamilton's financial measures but not that placing the capital on the Potomac achieved the opposite. Unlike the major capitals of Europe, from London to Rome, the economic and political centers of the new republic were separated from each other. The forces of decentralization, which sought to keep political power out of the hands of the moneymen while elevating the values of agrarian democracy, won a significant victory. The small new capital symbolized that this was not a grandiose government next door to, and presumably corrupted by, Wall Street. The isolation and size of the capital reflected the republican creed behind it. And in the coming century, when visitors asked for the location of the nation's capital—only to be informed that they were in the middle of it—that, too, was reassurance that this was not an overpowering central government that might strip away the rights and powers that the Constitution insisted were reserved to the states and the people.

Notes

1. Forrest McDonald, *Alexander Hamilton* (New York: W. W. Norton & Company, 1979), 181.

2. This account benefited from the very fine chapter "The Dinner," from Joseph J. Ellis, *Founding Brothers* (New York: Vintage Books, 2000).

3. See Ron Chernow, *Alexander Hamilton* (New York: The Penguin Press, 2004).

4. Samuel Eliot Morison and Henry Steele Commager, *The Growth of the American Republic*, Vol. 1 (New York: Oxford University Press, 1962), 332.

5. McDonald, 184.

6. Bob Arnebeck, *Through a Fiery Trial, Building Washington, 1790–1800* (New York: Madison Books, 1991), 20–24.

7. See Charlene Bangs Bickford and Kenneth R. Bowling, *Birth of the Nation: The First Federal Congress, 1789–1791* (Washington, DC: The First Federal Congress Project, 1989), Chapter IX, "Funding the Revolutionary War Debt."

8. For a comprehensive and lively treatment of the debates over locating the capital, see Kenneth R. Bowling, *The Creation of Washington, DC: The Idea and Location of the American Capital* (Fairfax, VA: George Mason University Press, 1991), Introduction.

9. Ellis, 70.

10. James Thomas Flexner, *Washington: The Indispensable Man* (Boston: Little, Brown and Company, 1974), 237.

11. Bowling, 110–111.

12. Bob Arnebeck, "Tracking the Speculators," *Washington History* 3, no. 1 (Spring/Summer 1991): 113–125.

13. C. M. Harris, "Washington's Gamble, L'Enfant's Dream: Politics, Design and the Founding of the National Capital," *William & Mary Quarterly*, 3rd Series, Vol. LVI, no. 3 (July 1999): 527.

14. Ellis, 49.

15. Ibid., 73–74.

16. Ibid., 76–77; Bowling, 201.

17. Bowling, 233.

18. Ulysses S. Grant was the president who firmly established the national capital's permanence. See Kenneth R. Bowling, "From 'Federal Town' to 'National Capital,'" *Washington History* 14, no. 1 (Spring/Summer 2002): 8–25.

19. Bowling, *The Creation of Washington, DC*, 224.

chapter 2

Federalism in Education
No Child Left Behind

When it came to accepting federalism, the framers of the Constitution didn't have much choice. The division of powers between the central and state governments was a given. In the framers' view, the decentralized confederation of states hadn't worked out very well, and it would have been politically unthinkable to ignore the states they represented to form a unified government. What emerged was a distribution of responsibilities, with those for the federal government written into the Constitution and the far more numerous ones remaining with the states, as stated clearly in the Tenth Amendment.

Since then, a system of cooperative federalism (more or less) has evolved. In these supportive relations the federal government provides funds to the states for policies set by Congress. Although generally lacking the ability to command the states, the federal government uses this money as a carrot (some call it a bribe) to meet Washington's standards or fulfill policy goals. For their part, the states maneuver to get national funds without having to follow the restrictions found in federal rules, formulas, or grant proposals. The result is a complicated system of "marble cake federalism," where intergovernmental relations have become so blurred that the line between where the federal government ends and where state and local administration begins is hard to trace—much like the swirls in a marble cake.[1]

Education has been traditionally overseen and funded on the local level, with support from the states. Since Lyndon Johnson's "War on Poverty" programs of the 1960s, the federal government has gotten increasingly involved in schools. The latest sign of this is the No Child Left Behind law, backed by the Bush administration and passed in 2002 with bipartisan support. The 1,000-page bill made the schools, their local districts, and the states accountable for student academic achievements. This standards-based reform required regular testing and qualified teachers in every classroom, and was supported by increased federal funds. In terms of federalism, it marked a strengthening of Washington's role in public education. What didn't change was the need to apply national policies to a variety of state and local conditions. It also didn't change the role of state and local officials in achieving, changing, blocking, or ignoring implementation of the law. In short, federalism remained alive and well, and central to whether No Child Left Behind would actually improve the public schools.

---

concepts highlighted

1. Federalism sets the boundaries of a **struggle for power** among national, state, and local governments. This case of education reform spotlights the history of this interaction, the politics involving elected officials, and the different educational bureaucracies implementing the reforms. What resources does each side bring to the control of education policies? How do state and local officials limit federal influence in education?

2. **Cooperative federalism** is the use of funds by the federal government to encourage (rather than command) states and localities to pursue national goals. How has the federal government used its money to gain state and local agreement for education changes in the past and No Child Left Behind at present? Considering that it contributes less than 10 percent of education monies, how successful has the federal government been?

3. The blurred distinction between the various governments in the creation and implementation of national programs has been called **marble cake federalism.** This lack of a clear dividing line in local, state, and federal government activities is evident in both passing and acting on No Child Left Behind, including test standards and teaching quality. Note how this surfaces in practical ways in the example of Kodiak Island schools.

4. The charge against the current education reform has been that it is an **unfunded mandate**—imposing national standards without providing adequate federal money to fulfill them. Look for education reforms, both past and present, where the federal government set out goals and requirements on the states without providing enough for the costs of the programs. Who is likely to make this argument in the battleground of federalism?

January 8, 2002, was as close as politicians get to a bipartisan pep rally. Four months after September 11, 2001, it was good to have something to cheer about and something other than terrorism to focus on. President George W. Bush, with applauding members of Congress on both sides of him and an equally happy crowd in front, was signing a major education reform bill, No Child Left Behind. The president described it as a "new era." Senator Edward Kennedy echoed Democrats' enthusiasm by calling it "a defining issue about the future of our nation."

Outside of Washington the cheers were not quite as loud. NCLB marked an unprecedented expansion of federal authority over the 50 states, 15,000 school districts, and their 80,000 public schools. NCLB established a federal system of school accountability, requiring states to develop standards in reading and math, and then testing students in seven grades on those standards. The new law required states to raise the qualifications for new teachers and certify the qualifications of current ones in the subjects they taught. The reform involved more testing, more standards, and more concentration on basics such as reading and math. If they met the new demands, lower-income school districts would receive additional federal funding, and all states and school districts would have greater flexibility in how they used this money. Despite the promise of more funds, anxiety could be expected among state and local education officials across the country.[2]

Not that there weren't real problems in public school education. The law addressed K–12 schooling (kindergarten through twelfth grade) where, despite a national average of just under $8,000 per child spent annually, there were widespread signs of failure. Some two-thirds of fourth graders could not read at grade level, and 88 percent of African American students and 85 percent of Hispanic students could not read proficiently. Even where the money seemed adequate, the results were not. (And this was in Congress's own backyard. The District of Columbia spent more than $13,000 per child, but it consistently ranked among the lowest national scores.) The new law, through its expanded testing, aimed to hold someone accountable for failure. Underscoring the point was that the unit being tested would no longer be only the school. Now test results would be measured by sex, race, income, limited English, and special education status. Each group would have to show gains in reading and math or make adequate yearly progress (AYP) toward agreed-on standards.

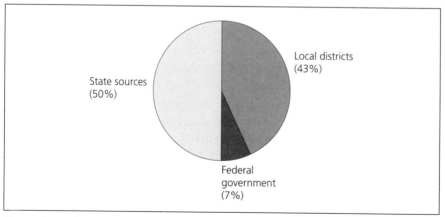

Figure 2.1 Education Spending Pie Chart: Federal, State, and Local Governments

Whether the federal government (still considered a "bit player" when it came to financing education—only 7 percent of the total costs of K–12) could get the leverage to guide the changes it wanted remained to be seen.[3]

A Primer on Federalism and Education

Issues of federalism have surfaced throughout the history of federal involvement in education and in the legislative crafting of No Child Left Behind, which climaxed four decades of federal expansion in this area.

Under President Lyndon Johnson, the 1965 Elementary and Secondary Education Act appropriated $2 billion to the states to improve education for the poor. This assistance to the states continued and increased over the next fifteen years. Then, in 1980, Ronald Reagan took office opposed to expanding Washington's role in education. Federal funding for education declined by 21 percent in the first five years of his administration. More positively, this conservative administration found that the education system was producing mediocre results and that higher academic standards needed to be established. This was left to the states. The result was that the states began implementing a variety of reforms that defined a core curriculum and the basic knowledge that students were expected to achieve at certain grade levels, called standards-based accountability. Some states also saw this as an unfunded mandate, with the federal government urging standards without providing the resources for achieving them.

Both of Reagan's successors, George H. W. Bush and Bill Clinton, provided federal funding to support state and local standards. The first President Bush set national education goals for the year 2000, including raising the high school graduation rate to 90 percent, requiring students to demonstrate competency in core disciplines, and making U.S. students the first in the world in science and mathematics scores. President Clinton built on these policies and attempted to gain authority for the federal government to approve or reject states' standards. Republicans, who took over Congress in 1994, strongly opposed this increased federal role, and Clinton later dropped it.

Despite this setback for federal oversight, the 1994 reauthorization of the Elementary and Secondary Education Act established the commitment to standards-based reform and holding the states accountable. The idea of "adequate yearly progress" was adopted, requiring the states to make progress toward goals of academic achievement for all students. However, neither deadlines nor penalties were put in place. Federal grants underlined this cooperative federalism by helping the states develop their own standards and tests. Although states kept autonomy over their education systems, to receive federal funds they had to fulfill some general requirements. The 1994 reauthorization was important in developing standards and tests in most states.[4] Equally important was that seven years later, only one-third of the states were complying with its requirements. This slow response would frustrate Washington's political leaders and lead to the bipartisan consensus behind No Child Left Behind.[5]

In 2001 George W. Bush took office and announced that education would be his number one domestic priority. Part of his thinking was formed by his experience as governor of Texas, where he supported annual testing and rating schools based on state exams. Another part was political. His Republican party had long been on the unpopular side of the education issue by pushing for cuts in spending while Democrats advocated more funds for schools. Running for president as a "compassionate conservative," Governor Bush had expressed sympathy for students trapped by "the soft bigotry of low expectations." His support for a strong federal role in education policy put him at odds with Republicans, who had traditionally stressed keeping the national government out of local schools. His political flexibility was shown in the very title of the legislation, taken from the liberal Children's Defense Fund, whose mission was "to leave no child behind."[6]

Borrowing from Clinton administration education plans, Bush introduced a thirty-page general blueprint in early 2001. Learning from Clinton's massive, and unsuccessful, 1993 health care reform bill, the Bush White House tried not to get bogged down in details. Although the plan was well received on Capitol Hill, federalism played a role in the politics of passing the bill. The states, represented by their governors, pushed for restraints on the federal government. They pressured the White House to weaken the bill's requirement that states must make adequate yearly progress among various groups of students. The fear was that many, or even most, schools would be identified as failing. They also tried to weaken the tests. To gain Democratic support for annual testing, Republicans eliminated vouchers that provided government funding for transferring students to private schools. Other compromises favorable to the states allowed school districts to average test results over three years and eliminated penalties for states with low test scores.

"Accountability" was the key, if vague, term unifying support in Congress for No Child Left Behind. For Democrats, it justified a reform that would increase spending for education. For Republicans, it gave the appearance of a businesslike approach to new investments in education. For the states, "accountability" meant "no national tests" and no binding enforcement by the federal government. There were no penalties for states not achieving adequate yearly progress. It was left to each state to define student achievement through its own tests, leaving open the possibility that the states could then lower standards. The viability of these muddy political compromises would be determined in their implementation. The blurred distinctions of this marble cake federalism left the fate of education reform in many different hands, on many levels of government.

Implementing Federalism: No Child Left Behind

Shortly after the bill passed Congress, *Education Week* interviewed officials in forty-five states and concluded that they generally supported the law, believing it mirrored the push for greater accountability taking place in many states. These state officials looked forward to new funding, worried about mandatory changes in their testing programs, and doubted they could hire the necessary highly qualified teachers. Asked whether his state could meet the law's time-table, the Colorado Commissioner of Education bluntly answered, "Will we have a qualified teacher in every classroom by 2005? No, of course not."[7]

In fairness, NCLB outlined a twelve-year program for education improve-ment, so it's still too early to draw conclusions on its impact. That hasn't kept numerous interests from weighing in on the law's negative consequences. Democrats have denounced the reform as an "unfunded mandate," requiring the states to meet certain goals (e.g., testing, hiring teachers) and then not giv-ing them the funds to pay for them. These complaints have given congres-sional Democrats and local officials who originally supported the law the en-couragement to criticize the administration. The argument has also been heard in states that have seen their budgets for education reduced by the re-cent recession. Administration supporters point out that federal education spending is more than $35 billion, that funds for primary and secondary schools have increased by 41 percent since 2001, and that the additional $14.5 billion that Bush has spent is not exactly an effort to starve public schools.[8]

State and local education officials have been under public pressure to boost their students' test scores. They have defended themselves by criticizing the business management practices in the law (such as strategic planning, stan-dardization, and data analysis) as robbing them of the flexibility needed to adapt to local education demands. "Teaching to the test" has been a feared re-sult of the emphasis on measuring student performance. State legislators de-nounced the bill, but only one state, Vermont, has passed a resolution stat-ing that local school districts are not required to spend their own money on No Child Left Behind. In North Carolina, where nearly three-quarters of the schools met their state test score goals, it was estimated that if federal standards had been in place only 27 percent of the state's schools would have passed.[9] Three towns in Connecticut turned down federal money for testing, saying that the money wasn't worth the trouble. While there were no federal consequences for not meeting adequate yearly progress in the test results, labeling schools as failing that were formerly well regarded was considered bad enough.[10]

What will the federal government do if states do not comply with the law? Using past behavior as a guide, many observers were skeptical that the Department of Education would actually force compliance. This passive acceptance could be a reasonable response to states that were making progress against difficult realities. It could also reflect the political difficulty (especially in the election year of 2004) of coming down hard on a powerful governor of the president's party—or even of the other party. While the department has demanded compliance, it recently revised the "highly qualified teacher" standard to give rural areas extra time to comply, relaxed deadlines covering the treatment of special education students, and issued changes in regulations called "flexibilities" in response to teachers' protests. Creative nudging rather than strong-arm tactics is the likely path in implementing the reform.[11] The following case demonstrates why the flexibility of cooperative federalism may be necessary in dealing with the unique difficulties local schools face.

North to Alaska: No Child Left Behind Comes to Kodiak

The Center on Education Policy, a nonpartisan think tank, commissioned fifteen case studies of local implementation of NCLB across the country. Completed at the beginning of the 2003–2004 school year, the studies provided an early look at the impact of the law. This is the case of Kodiak Island, Alaska.

Alaska's Kodiak Island is hardly a typical American school district. (But are schools in Chicago's inner city or in a wealthy Connecticut suburb or in dusty midlands Texas any more typical?) Kodiak does provide a pointed reminder of the difficulty in crafting national policies that can apply to widely differing local education needs and resources.

Located in the Gulf of Alaska, Kodiak serves nearly 3,000 students in the town and in native villages around the island. Half of Kodiak's students are white, and most of the rest are Alaska Natives and Asian-Pacific Islanders. Some 14 percent of the students are English language learners, with a diversity of languages and native dialects ranging from Japanese to Yupik. The challenge is to make students proficient in English as quickly as possible.

Five Kodiak schools did not meet AYP (annual yearly progress) levels in language and math. The subgroups that fell short in these schools were the English language learners and students with disabilities. The problems these groups have with the tests are not difficult to figure out. In the case of English learners, students are promoted out of the subgroup once they learn English, leaving behind those who are having trouble. Among students with disabilities, many were referred to special education precisely because they had significant learning problems. Not surprisingly they don't do well on state tests.

Schools in Kodiak, Alaska, have difficulty keeping qualified teachers.
Photo by Anna Nelson/Courtesy Port Lions School, Kodiak, Alaska

Schools in Kodiak run into unusual challenges. The rural district has difficulty attracting and keeping qualified teachers, resulting in a turnover of 30 to 50 percent each year. While adventurous souls are often drawn to teach in Alaska, most leave after one or two long winters. Learning to order groceries for an entire semester, watching out for bears when going outside, and battling loneliness all take their toll on teachers from outside the state.

This leads to depending on paraprofessionals, often Alaska natives, to provide much of the teaching in rural villages. Yet almost three-quarters of these paraprofessionals do not meet the NCLB definition of "highly qualified" teachers. Many teachers have not met the requirements for specific content areas, like math. Worse yet, to get the necessary credentials for some subjects requires going out of state for the degree. Sometimes a village school may have just one teacher and a paraprofessional covering twenty students in all twelve grades. How can one teacher meet NCLB standards for every subject he or she is teaching? How can the district find teachers for these schools with certificates in multiple disciplines? According to the Center on Education Policy case study, meeting this NCLB requirement is Kodiak's greatest challenge.[12]

Instructors who work to upgrade their skills must first overcome some formidable obstacles. They cannot go to school in the summer because the short warm season is when they hunt for deer and fish to feed their families during the long, harsh winter. Distance learning, by mail and computer, requires a lengthy commitment for paraprofessionals, who already have many family and village demands on their time. To meet this need for teachers, Kodiak is developing a broadband interactive learning program that will provide students with highly qualified teachers in subjects for which their regular teacher doesn't have certification. The plan is for the teacher who is, for instance, qualified in math to teach her own class while the lesson is transmitted to other schools for students who need the course. Kodiak is applying for a grant to fund this program.

State and local funding cuts have made these problems worse. The local schools have had significant budget reductions in recent years due to declining enrollment. State budget cuts have forced the schools to eliminate programs just when they're needed to meet NCLB goals. The district spending on education is at its maximum, with few alternatives to filling the gap left by state cuts other than reducing spending. The recent economic slumps in logging, fishing, and salmon canning industries have worsened the situation. With some classes enrolling 90 percent of children from low-income families, the students' outside jobs take on even more importance for their families in tough times. This leaves less time for homework, school activities, and preparing for a lot of new tests.

Even the NCLB provisions that require offering students the choice of another school would be difficult to carry out in the Alaskan setting. In a striking example of overlapping marble cake federalism, if their local school fails to provide progress toward certain education benchmarks, under No Child Left Behind, students can attend a different school at the expense of the district. In Alaska, however, this does not mean busing; it means putting children on an airplane! The U.S. Department of Education has recognized these special circumstances and has allowed schools in Alaska to offer supplemental services instead of school choice, at least for their first year.

Education, Coherence, and Federalism

Nine times nine is the same in any state.
Paul O'Neill

The federal government's modern role in public education began with a concern for those in greatest need. Federal dollars became "leadership dollars," with the goal of reforming education by closing the achievement gap between students of different races and developing programs based on scientific research. Although contributing less than a dime for every dollar spent on K–12 education, federal money has been vital in motivating change in the system.[13]

Under federalism, Washington has to operate through state agencies to change public education. The idea that the feds can dominate the system through their funds is clearly overstated—limited by a host of competing pressures, their own unwillingness to hurt children by cutting off money, and the political influence that local officials can exert through Congress. The result is a complex, multilayered, and often confused educational system. An ambitious reform like No Child Left Behind will ultimately succeed or fail based on countless negotiations at all levels of federalism.

Federalism has historically allowed local dominance in public education. It has not provided a coherent educational system of high standards, regular assessments of students and teachers, and accountability to the citizens paying for it. Local control has been an effective rallying cry in limiting changes to America's public schools. Whether it has produced world-quality education for the nation is another question entirely.

Notes

1. The term "marble cake federalism" comes from Morton Grodzins, "The Federal System," *Goals for Americans* (Englewood Cliffs, NJ: Prentice-Hall, 1960).
2. Andrew Rudalevige, "The Politics of No Child Left Behind," in Paul E. Peterson and Martin R. West, eds., *No Child Left Behind? The Politics and Practice of Accountability* (Washington, DC: The Brookings Institution Press, 2004).
3. Katherine Mangu-Ward, "No Demagogue Left Behind," *The Weekly Standard,* March 29, 2004.
4. See "History of the Federal Role in Education," *www.educationnext.org.*
5. Christopher T. Cross, *Political Education* (New York: Teachers College Press, 2004), 124.
6. From Rudalevige.
7. As quoted by Cross, *Political Education,* 141–142.
8. Brian Friel, "The Bush Record," *National Journal,* March 20, 2004, 869.
9. "Education Laws Work at Cross Purposes," *News & Record* (Greensboro, NC), October 27, 2002.
10. Jane Gordon, "Towns Are Rejecting No Child Left Behind," *New York Times,* December 21, 2003.
11. Brian Friel, "Damage Control for 'No Child Left Behind,'" *National Journal,* June 5, 2004, 1786.
12. Center on Education Policy, *Case Studies of Local Implementation of the No Child Left Behind Act,* "Alaska: Kodiak Island Borough School District," October 7, 2003. See the center's website: *www.cep-dc.org.*
13. See Cross, Chapter 9.

chapter 3

Affirmative Action at the University of Michigan

N early everyone has an opinion about affirmative action. These civil rights programs are designed to compensate for past discrimination and encourage future diversity. Although now applied to various ethnic groups and women, they originally focused on the rights of black Americans. The goals of these programs are to overcome injustices, but they often cause resentment between those favored and those left out.

The institutions of government, while seldom neutral, attempt to maintain a balance among competing claims. The courts are at the forefront in interpreting and applying policies in this arena of civil rights. They do so within the framework of the Constitution, relevant laws, and their own previous decisions. (And, as often noted, the justices read not only the Constitution but the newspapers as well.) The courts' historical record of reaching compromises without inciting violence among these conflicting "politics of rights" is a tribute both to the judges and to the groups' understanding that even the most cherished rights cannot be absolute.

In these cases covering admission to the college and law school of the University of Michigan, the Supreme Court struggled to find a balance. The two cases involved similar lawsuits filed by rejected white applicants. In one, *Gratz v. Bollinger,* the Court was asked to judge an admissions policy at the college that awarded bonus points for race. In the other, *Grutter v. Bollinger,* the Court reviewed the law school admissions policy that used race to promote educational diversity. The Court had to determine whether race-conscious admissions was a constitutional way to promote diversity and whether the Michigan programs were a flexible and limited means of doing so. In reaching its landmark decisions, the Court looked not only to legal principles for guidance, but to the evolving political views prevailing in the country.

concepts highlighted

1. **Equal opportunity versus equal outcome** sums up the conflicting positions toward affirmative action. The first stresses the historic tradition that individuals should be given the same chance to get ahead, whereas the second seeks some proportional share of benefits for a disadvantaged group. Does equality of outcome mean restricting the free competition—in hiring and admissions, for example—that lies behind equality of opportunity? Should some people be treated differently *now*—say, in admissions—to be treated equally in the future—for example, in grades?

2. Those objecting to the Michigan program contend that it results in **reverse discrimination**. This means that members of the majority do not get the same benefits—in this case admission to the university—that minority students do. Were the two women bringing the case victims of reverse discrimination? Were they also victims of discrimination in favor of athletes and children of alumni? Under the court rulings could they still claim to be at a disadvantage to favored groups?

3. **Preference policies** began as temporary measures, and one justice voiced the hope that affirmative action would not be needed in twenty-five years. These programs, however, have inevitably included formerly unprotected groups (such as women and people with disabilities) and encouraged politicians to expand the benefits. Do these policies promote group privileges and divisions? Can they be expected to disappear as prejudice declines?

4. The Court's decisions are an example of **judicial activism** in that they vigorously shape government policies in the conflicted area of civil rights. Notice how the justices, in their decisions and opinions, acted as policymakers, balancing objections to the programs while stressing the gains for society from affirmative action. In its rulings, did the Court act as a politically sensitive representative body or simply as judges interpreting the law?

Making the Case

60 Minutes correspondent Ed Bradley was interviewing an attractive blonde about how affirmative action had changed her life. Jennifer Gratz, who had brought a suit against the University of Michigan, described growing up in a Detroit suburb with dreams of attending college at Ann Arbor. She had a 3.8 grade point average, scored in the top 20 percent on her SATs, was a National Honor Society member, vice president of the student council, and a senior citizen helper. "But," concluded Bradley, "for the University of Michigan, it wasn't enough. She was rejected." Gratz told of her reaction to the news.

Barbara Grutter, left, and Jennifer Gratz, the two plaintiffs in the University of Michigan affirmative action cases.
Paul Sancya/AP–Wide World Photos

> I remember the day like it was yesterday. I came home from prac-
> tice, cheerleading practice, and grabbed the mail. And it was a thin
> envelope. And then I opened it, and I-I—I read probably the first
> three lines at that point and started crying. . . .

Gratz blamed affirmative action. A university spokesman denied that these policies led to her rejection, pointing out that many factors figured into every decision. Admissions awarded applicants points for various criteria. For example, a perfect GPA got 80 points, an alumni parent was worth 4 points, athletes were given 20 points, an outstanding essay merited 1, and being a minority was 20. A skeptical Bradley asked, "Is being a minority twenty times more important than writing an outstanding essay?"

Later in the show, Bradley talked with Tom Turner, a black student who grew up in poverty and had a difficult home life but managed to graduate high school with a mediocre record.

> I was a mid-C student at best. But the fact of the matter is, that since
> I've arrived at the University of Michigan, I've done far better than

my GPA or my SAT scores would have implied. . . . I'm a 3.9, Phi Beta Kappa, honor student in American culture now. Nobody could have possibly predicted that based on my high school scores or anything that came from high school.[1]

When asked about Gratz, Turner agreed that the process had not been fair to her.

It was reported on *60 Minutes* that the Center for Individual Rights had brought Gratz's suit against the undergraduate college as well as a parallel lawsuit for Barbara Grutter, who was rejected by the law school. CIR charged the university with violating both women's rights to equal treatment by giving unlawful preference to minorities in admissions. Funded by conservative foundations, CIR was a public interest law firm assisted by lawyers from established private firms who donated their services pro bono (at no charge). CIR had already won significant victories against affirmative action in California and Washington State. In selecting attractive test cases, the center had not just stumbled upon Gratz by chance, as this account from the *Washington Post* makes clear.

> When the group decided to sue, staffers pored over resumes and biographies of about 100 potential plaintiffs, information sent to them by sympathetic state legislators in Michigan. . . . The group's search for a camera-ready lead plaintiff ended when Gratz, a blonde homecoming queen from a blue-collar family, walked in the door. She had stellar grades, no apparent political leanings, and good looks to boot. CIR staffers tipped off the *New York Times* about her suit, and soon a long line of print and television journalists formed.[2]

Both *Gratz v. Bollinger* and *Grutter v. Bollinger* gave the Supreme Court an opportunity to deliver landmark decisions on affirmative action in June 2003.

Affirmative Action: The Debate

The seeds of affirmative action lay in the civil rights movement of the 1950s and 1960s. The argument has been made that affirmative action is a change in the goals of the early movement—from equalizing opportunity by removing discrimination to overcoming the consequences of discrimination by using compensating remedies. A simpler way to say it might be *equal opportunities versus equal results.* But as early as 1965 President Lyndon Johnson directed government agencies to hire minorities and minority-run companies. These efforts to correct racial inequities spread to private employment and college admissions, and they were pushed by the government, including Republican administrations like Richard Nixon's. Soon they also applied to women and disadvantaged ethnic groups not originally identified as benefiting from the programs. Quotas were used to guarantee these groups access to business, employment, and universities.

The rise of conservatives to national power in the 1980s accelerated opposition to affirmative action. Republicans took advantage of popular dissent toward the programs to shape a "wedge issue" that would divide black and white Democrats. Demands for a "color-blind society" were heard, often from the same voices that objected to this goal of equality when segregation was the law of the land. The political system, from state and local referendums to federal agency and court decisions, steadily chipped away at affirmative action. In response, advocates revamped the programs, following President Clinton's advice in his notable 1995 speech on the subject, "Mend It, Don't End It."[3] The debate, however, did not end.

On the pro side, supporters of affirmative action argue that programs are needed because simply removing barriers to advancement is not enough to help victims of historic discrimination. Equality in the law is a false promise for people who are unequal in education, income, and opportunities. Preference in hiring and education is needed until these groups achieve equality with the majority. Although opponents of affirmative action often quote Martin Luther King—"I have a dream that my four little children will one day live in a nation where they will not be judged by the color of their skin but by the content of their character"—King also said the following.

> It is impossible to create a formula for the future which does not take into account that our society has been doing something special *against* the Negro for hundreds of years. How then can he be absorbed into the mainstream of American life if we do not do something special *for* him now, in order to balance the equation and equip him to compete on a just and equal basis?[4]

In addition to a remedy for discrimination, there is another argument for diversity. We are a multiracial society, and our institutions, if they are to function effectively, must reflect that. Tolerance and a sense of community come from working, learning, and serving together. Minorities in leadership positions not only provide role models for others in these disadvantaged groups, but also give the institutions a credibility they otherwise wouldn't have. As one dean at UCLA's law school said, "Do you think in this day and age we would be justified—legally or morally—if we had the only public law school in the country without any black students?"[5]

Two students express their opinions outside as the Supreme Court issues its opinion inside.
Alex Wong/Getty Images

On the con side, critics charge that the programs violate a basic American principle: that people should be judged as individuals and not as members of a group. Whether it was discrimination *for* whites 100 years ago, or discrimination *for* blacks today, both policies look at race rather than individual talent. The argument that the law must be color conscious today so it may be color blind tomorrow suffers from the same flaw as foreign political leaders who "suspend" their constitution in order to "build" a stronger democracy. In fact, the opposite happens: Affirmative action inevitably promotes racial categories rather than diminishing them.[6]

Critics argue that these programs fail in practice as well as in theory. Their benefits inevitably go to those most able to take advantage of them. In higher education this means the main beneficiaries are middle-class African Americans, not the poor. Even those benefiting find themselves stigmatized as being incapable of "making it" on the basis of individual worth. By attempting to remedy past wrongs, the programs discriminate against those not belonging to the favored groups, increasing interracial tensions. Each side seeks selfish advantages in a game where one group's gain is another's loss. According to President Reagan's assistant attorney general for civil rights, William Bradford Reynolds, "What had started as a journey to reach the ideal of color blindness deteriorated into a nasty squabble among vying racial groups, each making stronger and stronger claims for its share of the affirmative action pie, not by reason of merit but solely on the grounds of racial or ethnic entitlement."[7]

Public opinion has listened to the debate and in recent years has shown some increasing support for affirmative action. In a poll taken for the Pew Research Center, support for affirmative action programs stood at 63 to 29 percent in May 2003 as opposed to being favored by 58 to 36 percent in 1995. In a CBS poll, also in 2003, some 53 percent favored such programs, and 39 percent opposed them. However, when asked if these programs were "fair," only 47 percent answered yes. This last question hints at a problem in polling on affirmative action: Responses often depend on how the question is framed. When speaking of minorities, if the words "preferential treatment" were used, opinion turned negative. In response to the statement "We should make every possible effort to improve the position of blacks and other minorities, even if it means *giving them preferential treatment*," only 24 percent answered yes, while 72 percent said no.[8]

Legal Principles at Michigan

Scarcely any political question arises in the United States that is not resolved sooner or later into a judicial question.

Alexis de Tocqueville

Given the disputes set off by affirmative action, it is no surprise that the courts soon got involved. In dealing with the issue of race in higher education, judges looked to the Constitution, specifically the Equal Protection Clause of the Fourteenth Amendment. It provides that "no state shall . . . deny to any person within its jurisdiction the equal protection of the laws." Ratified in 1868, three years after the Civil War ended, the Fourteenth Amendment's purpose was to protect newly freed slaves from southern governments. Since then, the principles underlying the amendment have taken on broader significance. For example, the Equal Protection Clause served as the legal foundation for desegregating public schools.

Equal protection is triggered when the government (in this case, the University of Michigan) classifies individuals by race. The Court first evaluates the purposes of the classifications made by the law or regulation. In the case of classification by race, the Court applies the highest, most skeptical level of review, which is called "strict scrutiny." Under strict scrutiny the Court only allows racial classifications if they pass two criteria: (1) they are narrowly tailored, and (2) they further compelling government interests. Thus, race-conscious admissions programs that classify applicants by race are subject to strict scrutiny. Although the Court will not automatically invalidate these racial classifications, any higher-education admissions must pass through the screens of being narrowly tailored and needed to achieve a compelling interest. In the two cases before the Court, diversity in Michigan's student body had to be shown to be a sufficiently compelling interest. Would the university's policies fit?

The Court had its own precedents to follow in weighing the programs. Chief among them was the 1978 case *Regents of the University of California v. Allan Bakke.* Here a state's medical school had rejected a white student at the same time it had reserved 16 of the 100 places in its entering class for members of minority groups. In its 5 to 4 decision, the Court rejected this system of admissions as a quota and ordered Bakke admitted. But the majority opinion written by Justice Lewis Powell endorsed the goal of student diversity in higher education as a compelling government interest. Powell's opinion in *Bakke* had kept affirmative action alive. Now, a generation later, the issue was whether the Court would prohibit or allow the continued widespread use of race in admissions.

Gratz and Grutter filed their lawsuits late in 1997, challenging race-based admissions. Both charged that preferences for black, Hispanic, and Native American applicants violated the Equal Protection Clause of the Fourteenth Amendment. For the next several years the cases bounced around the federal court system—district courts as well as courts of appeal. In March 2001 a federal district court struck down the law school's race-based admissions system, finding that a diverse student body was *not* a compelling governmental interest. Further, the policy was not narrowly tailored to serve that interest because it was "indistinguishable from a straight quota system." The university appealed, and the Sixth Circuit Appeals Court agreed to hear both cases.

A deeply divided Sixth Circuit reversed the district judge's decision in May 2002. A 5 to 4 majority found that the law school's race-based admissions program was narrowly tailored to further a compelling governmental interest in diversity. No decision was issued in Gratz. The women's attorneys appealed, and in December 2002 the Supreme Court agreed to hear both Grutter and Gratz. The Court heard oral arguments in the two University of Michigan cases on April 1, 2003.

The Supreme Court Listens

Groups outside the case made sure they were heard. A record number of briefs signed by organizations and individuals were filed: seventy-eight in support of affirmative action and nineteen opposed. Their significance went beyond mere numbers. An astute observer of the Court (Linda Greenhouse, reporter for the *New York Times*) noted, "What is most striking is the range and sheer weight of the establishment voices on the affirmative action side." This "establishment" meant the nation's leading law schools, including the alma maters of every member of the Court, dozens of Fortune 500 companies such as General Motors and Microsoft, and professional associations, including the American Bar Association. Unexpectedly important were twenty-one retired generals and admirals, including three former military academy superintendents. Their conclusion, mentioned later by several justices, stated, "At present, the military cannot achieve an officer corps that is both highly qualified and racially diverse" without affirmative action. That an integrated officer corps was deemed essential to national security could not be dismissed lightly in post-9/11 America.[9]

The Bush administration opposed the university with a public posture stronger than its legal stance. President Bush took to TV shortly before filing the administration brief to present an image to his conservative supporters of resistance to affirmative action. In its actual filing at midnight the next day ("a fading second-day story"), the brief denounced the Michigan system as an unconstitutional quota system. If the university wanted diversity, it could use race-neutral programs like the plan at the University of Texas, which offered admission to students graduating in the top 10 percent of every high school in the state. However, the brief did not ask the Court to prohibit *any* use of race in college admissions, nor did it ask that the *Bakke* decision be overturned. This was a more realistic argument to make to the Court—what one professor called a signal "for what's do-able."[10]

In their presentations both sides followed their well-honed arguments. The plaintiffs, Gratz and Grutter, challenged the university's affirmative action policy as unlawfully discriminating against them by taking race into account as a "plus" factor in admissions. The university maintained that the Constitution allowed it to use race and ethnicity to achieve the educational benefits of a diverse student body. Diversity was the "compelling governmental interest" justifying the use of racial categories in admissions. Then the justices began firing questions at the lawyers.

Justice Ruth Bader Ginsburg asked the university's opponents if the race preference programs at the military academies were illegal. The lawyer for the plaintiffs dodged: "We haven't examined that. . . ." Questioning the other side, Justice Antonin Scalia complained that Michigan had brought the problem on itself by creating an elite law school. They could achieve diversity by making the state school less "exclusive." "Why have a super-duper law school?" asked the justice, a graduate of Harvard Law School. The university's attorney replied, "I don't think there's anything in this court's cases that suggests that the law school has to make an election between academic excellence and racial diversity." Justice Sandra Day O'Connor, expected to be the crucial swing vote, asked the plaintiffs' counsel whether he was saying that race "can't be a factor at all." His response: "Race itself should not be a factor among others in choosing students, because of the Constitution." O'Connor's objection hinted at the decision that lay ahead: "You are speaking in absolutes, and it isn't quite that."[11]

The Court Decides

On June 23, 2003, the U.S. Supreme Court ruled on the cases. It permitted the law school's admissions challenged by Grutter, but ruled against the undergraduate system in the Gratz suit. In both cases the Court found that diversity was a compelling interest in higher education that could justify race as a plus factor in admissions. The Court felt it should give some deference to universities when they made educational decisions on the benefits from diversity. In Grutter, the Court approved of the individualized review used by the law school in admissions, finding it was narrowly tailored to achieve diversity. Race could be used as one of several factors in evaluating each applicant. The law school's use of admissions to produce a critical mass of underrepresented minority students did not change a flexible program into a rigid quota. The vote by the Court was 5 to 4, with Justice O'Connor writing the Grutter opinion.

Michigan's undergraduate admissions did not do so well. In Gratz (a 6 to 3 decision, with Justice O'Connor again in the majority), Chief Justice Rehnquist held that the automatic distribution of twenty points to students from minority groups was not narrowly tailored. By not considering other individual merits in awarding the points, the system made race decisive for "virtually every minimally qualified underrepresented minority applicant." This had to change. Despite the administrative difficulties, admissions should provide an individualized review of what each applicant might contribute to the diversity of the entering class. This included factors other than race and meant that all candidates should be competing against the entire pool, not just against members of the same racial group. Any system should impose the smallest possible burden on non-minority students.[12]

In its opinions, the Court provided a blueprint for considering race without violating the Constitution's guarantee of equal protection. The key issue was whether the programs were narrowly tailored: The college's twenty-point formula wasn't; the individualized law school process was. Flexibility was a theme in the Court's decisions. Both opinions indicated that race *can* be a factor, not that it *must* be. Programs that prohibited the use of race in states like California and Washington were allowed to continue.

The emotions and the divisions within the Court were strikingly captured by Justices Sandra Day O'Connor and Clarence Thomas. Writing for the majority in the Grutter case, Justice O'Connor saw a broad national consensus in favor of affirmative action in higher education. Clearly influenced by the many briefs from the country's leading institutions, she concluded that affirmative action's benefits were real, not theoretical, and were still needed in business, the military, and universities. The Court's job was reactive: to reflect and support this political consensus behind building a more equal society.

Justice Thomas's dissent was more personal. He criticized affirmative action as a "cruel farce of racial discrimination." The Court's lone African American justice and an accomplished graduate of Yale Law School, Thomas accused Michigan's law school of tantalizing unprepared students with the promise of a degree. Only later would they discover that they could not succeed against the competition. "The majority of blacks are admitted to the law school because of discrimination, and because of this policy all are tarred as undeserving." Who can tell who belongs and who does not? The question itself, Thomas concluded, stigmatizes black students as "otherwise unqualified."[13]

Reaction and Impact

The first reaction to the Court's decision was a sigh of relief from the civil rights communities. The possibility that this conservative Court—which had in the past emphasized the limits of affirmative action—might further restrict these programs had been a real concern. The new president of the University of Michigan considered the rulings among the Court's great landmark decisions, providing universities with a "green light" to pursue diversity. More surprising was the praise from the White House. President Bush commended the Court for "recognizing the value of diversity on our nation's campuses." His statement did not mention that he had asked the Court to throw out both Michigan programs as thinly disguised quota systems.[14]

Some conservatives found reasons to be pleased by the decisions. The head of CIR, the firm that had filed the lawsuits, stressed the blow to the college admissions point system. He said, "The ruling is a mixed decision that signals the beginning of the end of race-based preferences in America." Carl Cohen, a Michigan professor who had led the charge against his university's admissions policies, wasn't surprised that the court accepted the "mushier wording" of the law school while rejecting "the mechanical and blatantly discriminatory" undergraduate system.[15] Another lawyer from CIR pointed to Justice O'Connor's hope that affirmative action should "no longer be necessary" twenty-five years from now. The attorney concluded, "The court says affirmative action is not timeless, and it had better not be."[16]

Colleges tended to be cautious in their reaction. In practice, the rulings upholding race-conscious admissions made it more expensive and complicated for them. Nor could the colleges assume that the Court had ended further legal threats. Race could no longer be the sole factor governing a college's decisions. Only one-third of colleges, generally the most selective, had race-conscious admissions policies. But these colleges had to reexamine recruiting programs for minorities in high schools, ethnically separate student housing, and financial aid. Even the accepted goal of promoting diversity for educational reasons had a double edge to it. One college was advised not to use the term "underrepresented minority" because that would imply that the college was trying to produce minority enrollments that represented the general population. This was a different goal from having a "critical mass" of minority students to provide the educational benefits of diversity.[17]

To the Future

Although divisions persisted on affirmative action, the response to the Michigan decisions showed that some of the bitterness of the past had moderated. Consideration of race in hiring and admissions was broadly accepted, if not welcomed. The consequence of this inclusion was to choose racial justice over color blindness, to equalize society's institutions even by sacrificing individual equality. That there were benefits to both the universities and the minorities affected has become increasingly acknowledged.[18] Between 1972 and 1996 the percentage of blacks enrolling in college immediately after high school rose from 44.6 to 56 percent. Law school enrollment grew from 1 percent black in 1960 to 7.5 percent in 1995.[19]

Yet these programs were judged by the courts on their benefits to the educational institution, not to the minorities involved. The courts' discussion of affirmative action in university admissions largely ignored whether these programs have improved minority or working-class education in this country. And here the argument continues. One recent study found that black law students admitted to elite law schools were more likely to drop out, or to graduate but fail their bar exams. The statistical study concluded that many black students were "victims" of racial preferences that placed them in schools which they were not academically prepared for and where they performed badly.[20]

The real racial division may lie in public education before college, a system where only one in five minority students graduate from high school with the bare minimum qualifications to even apply to college. To attend college, students must have graduated from high school, taken a set of required courses, and demonstrated basic literacy. Of the country's 1.2 million black and Hispanic eighteen-year-olds only some 218,000 can be considered college ready.

Virtually all of these students attend college. The main challenge for the future lies not in expanding opportunities in higher education but in improving public schools so that more minority students are given the skills they need to attend college.[21]

The charge that diversity in higher education has only meant *racial* diversity has begun to be taken seriously at the nation's top colleges. A former Princeton president called these schools "bastions of privilege" and pointed out that only about 3 percent of a recent entering class at nineteen elite colleges were from lower-income families in which neither parent attended college. He argued that affirmative action admission preferences should be given to low-income students of any race as well as for minorities.[22]

As for the women plaintiffs whose names were on the lawsuits, neither seemed pleased with the outcome. In the years that it had taken their cases to reach the Supreme Court, both had continued their education elsewhere. Barbara Grutter, who had decided against law school after her initial rejection and gone on to study business, denounced the ruling as a smokescreen for illegal quotas. Jennifer Gratz, after being turned down, graduated from Michigan's satellite campus in Dearborn and moved to California. Following the decision she returned to a Detroit suburb to become executive director of the Michigan Civil Rights Initiative. Her group aimed to go around the Court's decision by passing a voter initiative similar to the one in California. Through that initiative, the state could ban racial preferences at public agencies, including admission to universities.[23]

Notes

1. Both the Gratz and Turner quotes are from "Negative About Affirmative Action?" anchor Ed Bradley, *60 Minutes* (CBS News Broadcast, October 29, 2000).
2. *Washington Post*, February 20, 1998, quoted by Lee Cokorinos, *The Assault on Diversity* (New York: Rowman & Littlefield Publishers, 2003), 63–64. Sponsored by the Institute for Democracy Studies, this is a critical look at conservative legal attacks on affirmative action.
3. A copy of the speech can be found in George E. Curry, ed., *The Affirmative Action Debate* (Reading, MA: Addison-Wesley, 1996), 258–276.
4. As quoted by Christopher Edley, Jr., *Not All Black and White* (New York: Hill and Wang, 1996), 85.
5. As quoted by Christopher Shea, "Under UCLA's Elaborate System Race Makes a Big Difference," in Robert Emmet Long, ed., *Affirmative Action* (New York: H. W. Wilson Company, 1995), 89.
6. Carl Cohen, as quoted by Richard F. Tomasson et al., *Affirmative Action: The Pros and Cons of Policy and Practice* (Washington, DC: American University Press, 1996), 117.

7. William Bradford Reynolds, "An Experiment Gone Awry," in Curry, 133.

8. Pew Research Center, "Conflicted Views of Affirmative Action," News Release, May 14, 2003. CBSNews.com, "Poll: U.S. Favors Affirmative Action," April 1, 2003.

9. Linda Greenhouse, "Affirmative Reaction: Can the Justices Buck What the Establishment Backs?" *New York Times,* Week in Review, March 30, 2003.

10. Linda Greenhouse, "Bush and Affirmative Action: Muted Call in Race Case," *New York Times,* January 17, 2003.

11. Linda Greenhouse, "Justices Look for Nuance in Race-Preference Case," *New York Times,* April 2, 2003.

12. Summaries of the court decisions can be found at *www.umich.edu/~urel/admissions/overview/.*

13. Linda Greenhouse, "The Justices: Context and the Court," *New York Times,* June 25, 2003.

14. Linda Greenhouse, "Justices Back Affirmative Action by 5 to 4, But Wider Vote Bans a Racial Point System," *New York Times,* June 24, 2003.

15. Janet Miller, "Court Ruling Draws Applause Across Much of U-M Campus," *Ann Arbor News,* June 24, 2003.

16. Greenhouse, "Justices Back Affirmative Action."

17. Peter Schmidt, "Affirmative Action Remains a Minefield, Mostly Unmapped," *Chronicle of Higher Education* 50, no. 9 (October 24, 2003): A22.

18. This positive case for affirmative action is exhaustively made by William G. Bowen and Derek Bok, *The Shape of the River* (Princeton, NJ: Princeton University Press, 1998).

19. From Gary Orfield and Dean Whitla, "Diversity and Legal Education," *Diversity Challenged,* Harvard Education Publishing Group, 2001.

20. The study is that of Richard Sander, a UCLA Law School professor. Stuart Taylor, "Do Racial Preferences Reduce the Number of Black Lawyers?" *National Journal,* December 4, 2004, 3583–3584.

21. Jay P. Greene and Greg Forster, "College Diversity: Fix the Pipeline First," *Washington Post,* January 7, 2004.

22. Amy Argetsinger, "Nudging the Needy into Nation's Top Colleges," *Washington Post,* April 13, 2004.

23. David Runk, "Woman Who Challenged U. of Michigan's Affirmative Action Policy to Lead Ballot Campaign," Associated Press State & Local Wire, January 12, 2004.

chapter 4

Freedom of Speech and Campus Speech Codes

The right to speak one's mind is basic to democracy and to a university. Most Americans would agree with that statement as a general endorsement of freedom of speech. Problems arise, however, when controversial ideas are expressed and people are offended. Further complicating the issue is that the courts have expanded the term *speech* to include symbolic actions like flag burning, and groups have expanded the concept of "fighting words," turning this form of speech into conduct verging on a physical attack. The division between words and actions summed up by the comment "Your right to swing your arm ends at the tip of my nose" does not distinguish words and actions as clearly today as it did when the Bill of Rights was first adopted. Some now believe that the tip of one's ego defines the limit of a verbal assault.[1]

In a sense, on college campuses, civil liberties have collided with civil rights. As universities have admitted more diverse student bodies, they have had to question many of their traditional ideas about education and speech allowed in the academic community. Feminists charge sexual harassment when a law professor lectures on how to question rape victims; gay rights groups are offended when a student describes homosexuality as a disease to be treated medically; and minorities protest when a DJ tells a racist joke on the college radio station. Can the principle of open discussions of controversial issues be maintained? Will diverse groups feel welcomed in the academic community? What will be the impact on a university's educational goals?

Speech codes (often appearing in "student conduct codes") have evolved as one answer. While paying homage to the principle of free speech, these codes attempt to discourage speech that could be considered offensive to a particular group. However well intended, when under "sexual harassment" a code prohibits "remarks of a sexual nature" and 'jesting' and 'kidding' about sex or gender-specific traits," it invites problems of interpretation.[2] The vagueness of such codes and the awkwardness of their implementation have led some universities to adopt less ambitious, more traditional approaches. Many educators argue that speech is better governed by courts that are guided by legal precedents and the

First Amendment. That, in turn, would allow universities to return to their educational mission of seeking knowledge through the widest possible discourse. This is not exactly a modest goal.

concepts highlighted

1. America's **marketplace of ideas** is a widely embraced value. Here opinions compete with one another to determine which will flourish and which will not. Although determined by the "hidden hand" of the market, the free expression that allows this competition merits legal protection. But how valid is this ideal? Does government intervention, opinion shaping by the media, and university guidelines make this hands-off ideal less than realistic? Therefore, shouldn't the consequences of speech be a reasonable way to judge the suitability of such expression on campus?

2. The San Diego and Shippensburg examples are attempts by universities to protect vulnerable students from harassment, even at the cost of limiting expression. The desire of some students for freedom clashes with that of others who want to be treated equally. Is this a case of **civil liberties versus civil rights**? Is this an unbridgeable division, or can the open exchange of ideas on a college campus be used to promote both?

3. **Fighting words** cause injury or incite an immediate breach of the peace. They are recognized by the courts and minority groups as different from ordinary speech. Without getting into the legal arguments, does such a concept make sense on college campuses? Should the affirmative action bake sales or the anti-Semitic speaker fall under this category and therefore be banned?

4. Do universities have **valid educational purposes** for limiting expression on campus? Should colleges meet a higher standard before being allowed to restrain expression? Or should this be part of the duties of a community of scholars policing ideas to weed out those with no redeeming intellectual purpose?

Universities and Speech

If there is a bedrock principle underlying the First Amendment, it is that the Government may not prohibit the expression of an idea simply because society finds the idea itself offensive or disagreeable.

Justice William J. Brennan, *Texas v. Johnson*, 1989

(In decision upholding flag-burning protest)

The events of September 11, 2001, led to a strange incident in the library of San Diego State University. Zewdalem Kebede, an Ethiopian-born student, overheard a discussion

in Arabic among three Saudi Arabian students sitting in the university library on Sep-
tember 22, 2001. According to Kebede, they were expressing delight at the success of the
terrorist attacks. Kebede, a naturalized American, became furious, confronted them in
Arabic, and told them that they "should feel shame" at the inhumane actions of their
compatriots. When a fourth student joined the discussion and asked Kebede if he was
threatening them, he said no and went back to his own table.

A few days later the university's Center for Student Rights and Responsibilities
charged Kebede with misconduct. He was threatened with suspension under a Califor-
nia Code of Regulations prohibiting "abusive behavior directed toward, or hazing of, a
member of the campus community." Kebede was forced to explain his actions in writing
to an administrator. He was put on probation and warned in a letter, "You are ad-
monished to conduct yourself as a responsible member of the campus community in the
future." A university spokesperson explained, "[We] feel we have to protect students
from feeling threatened."

A civil liberties group protested the university's action, pointing out that the state code
was directed toward physical abuse such as hazing and not impassioned speech. The
so-called victims outnumbered Kebede four to one, and the university silenced some stu-
dents' beliefs over others. The group asked whether universities wanted to put their
students in fear of reprisals for discussing controversial issues.[3]

The right to free speech would seem to be indispensable at a university. What is an ideal university if not a marketplace of ideas, allowing the most open, most free exchange of beliefs and opinions? Communicating knowledge and learning ought to demand unrestricted openness.

In reality, universities have some widely accepted restraints on freedom of expression. In some instances the campus is more restrictive than general society. Plagiarism is a striking example, reflecting the scholars' duty to credit others' research and ideas. The penalties for its violation are higher in academia than they are in the outside world, reflecting the university's special interest in the integrity of scholarship. Similarly, lying—a violation of many student honor codes—will mean sanctions from the university community, including expulsion, far harsher than anywhere else. These values and practices in defense of the university's mission are designed to produce standards of behavior higher than those of society at large.

A university's mission may also lead to greater protection for speech. Academic freedom is the university's traditional safeguard for what professors, and others, say and write in the classroom and even outside class. Such speech goes to the heart of academia's pursuit of truth. Academic freedom is a unique protection offered at most campuses. It prohibits punishments, such as job loss, for expression at universities, and this heightened defense of speech has been recognized by the courts.

Whether the institution is public or private affects the freedom of expression that's allowed. Private colleges and universities are generally freer to set their own limits on speech. For example, a church-affiliated school may set standards on student speech (e.g., blasphemy) that are stricter than what is acceptable in the off-campus world. But public universities are governed by the Constitution, whereas the courts give private universities a bit more flexibility. Administrators at these tax-supported academies are treated as agents of the government and are restrained by the First Amendment in their ability to limit campus speech. This led to their speech codes that restricted racist, sexist, or homophobic speech being consistently struck down by the courts as abridging constitutional freedoms. It happened recently in Pennsylvania.[4]

Restraining Speech and Speech Codes

Shippensburg University, a small public college in central Pennsylvania, published a "Code of Conduct" similar to those of other colleges. It gave each student a "primary" right to be free from harassment, intimidation, physical harm, or emotional abuse, and a "secondary" right to express personal beliefs in a manner that did not "provoke, harass, demean, intimidate, or harm" another. The university prohibited conduct that "annoys, threatens, or alarms a person or group" like sexual harassment, comments, insults, propositions, jokes about sex or gender-specific traits, and even "suggestive or insulting sounds," leering, whistling, or obscene gestures. Campus demonstrations and rallies were limited to two "speech zones."

Attorneys for a civil liberties nonprofit association, the Foundation for Individual Rights in Education (FIRE), filed a lawsuit against Shippensburg as part of its nationwide campaign against speech codes. FIRE charged that the code had a "chilling effect" on students' right to open discussions. The code made constitutionally protected free speech depend on the reaction of the most sensitive student. FIRE officials said that under this policy a student who accused Republicans of engaging in a racist war could be punished, as would a feminist who went to a rally with a sign reading "Keep your rosaries off my ovaries." The university responded that it "strongly and vigorously defends the right of free speech," adding that it expected students to "conduct themselves in a civil manner that allows them to express their opinions without interfering with the rights of others."

On September 4, 2003, a U.S. District Court judge issued a preliminary injunction ordering the university not to enforce its speech code. The judge concluded that the code was an attempt to achieve a "utopian community" but that good intentions did not justify censorship. Instructing students to apply the university's ideals of "racial toler-

*ance, cultural diversity, and social justice" was found by the court to be clearly uncon-
stitutional. Early in 2004, Shippensburg agreed to rewrite its speech policies as an
unenforceable university statement of values that did not restrict student expression in
any way.*[5]

The well-intended motives behind college speech codes are not questioned,
even by opponents. In the late 1980s, the Carnegie Foundation surveyed university presidents and reported that more than half of them considered racial
intimidation or harassment a serious problem on their campuses. The college
heads could provide many examples of students fulfilling the comic Groucho
Marx's goal for college: "We want to build a university our football team can be
proud of."

- At the University of Wisconsin–Madison, a giant racist caricature announced
  an on-campus party.
- A college fraternity put on a skit featuring jokes that mocked gay and les-
  bian lifestyles.
- A University of Michigan student posted a story on the Internet about tor-
  turing his female classmate with a hot curling iron.
- Two women at a California junior college protested the sexist comments
  posted on a men-only campus computer bulletin board.

There are several arguments for speech codes. One is that simply con-
demning racist, sexist, and homophobic statements in these codes might reduce how often they occur. The codes serve as a symbol that the university
will not tolerate such prejudice, thus providing a more comfortable environment for its students who might feel victimized. Banning offensive language is
viewed as a way of preserving the best values of academic dialogue and preventing contamination from comments with no redeeming social purpose. A
constitutional scholar argued that concepts like genocide should not even be
given the chance of acceptance in the marketplace of ideas, since such evil
thoughts could possibly be implemented in a democracy. Why wait to prevent
them only when they begin to be acted on? "Where nothing is unspeakable,
nothing is undoable."[6]

Few universities have worked to curb speech with any enthusiasm. Speech
codes arose during a period of change when administrators were responding
to troubling situations. Colleges were adapting to the admission of new ethnic
and racial groups by changing a campus climate that was often exclusive and
uncivil and to satisfy the outraged victims of discrimination. Racist and abusive
speech was seen as a pattern of behavior that interfered with learning and was
contrary to the educational values of the university. The case was put this way:

"What many speech code advocates are seeking is simple: a way of enlisting a whole community in creating an environment where people are not attacked and injured on the basis of their identity."[7]

Baking Brownies and Freeing Speech

It is by the goodness of God that in our country we have three unspeakably precious things: freedom of speech, freedom of conscience, and the prudence never to practice either of them.

Mark Twain

In the fall of 2003 conservative student organizations held "affirmative action bake sales" at colleges across the country. The sign that listed the prices of baked goods showed lower prices for black and Hispanic customers than for Asian and white customers. Supporters described the sales as political satire designed to draw attention to the unfairness in universities' affirmative action policies transferred to the absurdly petty level of a bake sale—and thus to spark debate about them.

The reaction was decidedly mixed. At William & Mary, the president denounced the bake sale as "inexcusably hurtful" and "abusive." The sale was halted because it "did not meet the administrative requirements we routinely impose on such activities." A lawyer for the student group remarked, "One can hardly imagine such tactics being used to shut down a protest that administrators found more to their liking politically."[8] At the University of Washington, the College Republicans holding the sales were assaulted. Students tore down the signs and threw cookies on the ground. Campus police intervened and, following administration orders, halted the bake sale. At Southern Methodist University, administrators shut down the Young Conservatives of Texas's bake sale after forty-five minutes because "some folks felt harassed by this discriminatory menu."

Other universities allowed the student bake sales. An Indiana University administrator resisted pressure to punish bake sale organizers, saying, "This is one of the more significant social and political issues of our time. . . . It is exactly the kind of dialogue that should be encouraged on college campuses." Bake sales protests occurred without official opposition at the University of Texas-Austin and at Texas A&M. At William & Mary, after press coverage, a second bake sale was allowed two months after the first one was halted. The William & Mary administration denied having acted improperly in stopping the previous protest.[9]

There are two basic arguments against speech codes: One is that this restriction on free speech violates the Constitution at public universities and violates

Pricing cookies based on the buyer's ethnicity, gender, and social status, these college Republicans at the University of California, Berkeley, cooked up a free speech issue.
Marcio José Sanchez/AP–Wide World Photos

the stated missions of private universities as well. The second is that speech codes prevent open discussion of ideas and are inappropriate for a university. Students cannot be expected to defend principles of free speech after they graduate if they are educated in a place where rights are granted or withheld depending on the whims of those in charge.

The constitutional argument is bolstered by the fairly consistent refusal of courts to support the restraints on speech in these codes. Judges have seen campus codes as interfering with protected First Amendment speech. Universities' attempts to rewrite codes—often putting them under the category of "student conduct"—and make them less sweeping have generally proven unsuccessful. Many campuses have given up attempting to comply with the courts' broad First Amendment rulings and have allowed their codes to fade into history. Speech codes, however, are still used in hundreds of universities.

The educational argument behind speech codes is that there are some expressions so contrary to the goals of a university that they should be banned. At various times in American history the restriction of certain ideas from universities—whether Marxism or atheism—has prevailed, much to the later embarrassment of the academic community. The problem of defining exactly what speech should be sanctioned has bedeviled the drafting of all speech codes. That may be because making some messages off limits sets a precedent of prohibiting thought. It empowers controversial ideas, implying that they cannot be presented because they cannot be countered through the normal methods of reason and debate. By punishing expression, the codes violate Thomas Jefferson's goal for a university as a place where error is allowed "so long as reason is free to pursue it. . . ."[10]

The university's special commitment to freedom of speech does not mean it should protect misconduct. Free speech advocates do not dispute the need to prevent threats or harassment directed at an individual or to keep classes from being disrupted. They argue, however, that sanctions should relate to conduct and not translate to vague restrictions on expression. Certain groups should not need special protection from certain words. Courts have upheld the idea that speech is not absolute, but the legal restrictions are very narrowly defined. Many university speech codes regulate expression that is clearly protected under the law. A former president of the University of California said, "The university is not engaged in making ideas safe for students. It is engaged in making students safe for ideas."[11] Exceptions to the general rule of protecting speech at a university ought to be just that—exceptions.

Universities and Talking

At Howard University in Washington, DC, a speaker at a Nation of Islam rally led a crowd of one thousand in the following call-and-response.
  Who controls the Federal Reserve?
  Jews!
  You're not afraid to say it, are you?
  Jews! Jews!
  Who controls the media and Hollywood?
  Jews!
  Who has our entertainers, our athletes, in a vise grip?
  Jews!
  Am I lying?
  No!
  One of those who was stunned by this expression of bias was Vera Katz, a Jewish teacher of acting at Howard. In her classes the next day, she discussed stereotypes and said, "Look at me! You know me! Am I a bloodsucker?" She told her students how hurt she was that her heritage had been assailed at the rally. She described their reactions.

They had to see me as a human being. They had to realize they were being taught by a Jewish lady who had been devoted to teaching students at Howard for a quarter of a century.

Her students responded that it was wrong to blame a whole group for the acts of a few: "Like how all African Americans often get indicted on the news programs for what only some African Americans do." One student complained that, as a show of solidarity, some black students felt they had to go along with anti-Semitism. Another commented to a newspaper that Professor Katz "comes from a very honest place," so that made him more open to her criticism. In other words, this teacher used her sincere reaction to bigotry and her right to speak to open rather than close minds.[12]

Much of what goes on at a university has been described as a conversation. It is a forthright discussion between teachers and teachers, teachers and students, and students and students. It is about debating and confronting controversial ideas, and challenging authority by learning to present evidence and arguments. It is a conversation that arouses emotions, provides a sanctuary for cranks and crackpots, and often seems pointless, futile, and wrong.[13] It is, however, talk, and a clear boundary between protected speech and prohibited conduct must be established on campus. The essence of a campus is a broad, engaging, and thriving conversation. Censor it, and you've removed something basic to education.

Notes

1. Alan Charles Kors and Harvey A. Silverglate, *The Shadow University* (New York: The Free Press, 1998), 84.

2. For an example, see the guidelines from the University of Maryland at *www.speech codes.org/*.

3. FIRE Case Archive, October 24, 2001, at *www.thefire.org*. Also Lou Marano, "School Warns Man Who Rebuked Saudis," United Press International, October 25, 2001.

4. Robert M. O'Neil, *Free Speech in the College Community* (Bloomington: Indiana University Press, 1997), "Introduction."

5. *The FIRE Quarterly* 1, no. 3-4 (Winter 2003); *The FIRE Quarterly* 2, no. 1 (Spring 2004).

6. Martin P. Golding, *Free Speech on Campus* (Boulder, CO: Rowman & Littlefield, 2000). Quote is from Alexander M. Bickel, 34.

7. O'Neil, 3–7.

8. FIRE News, "FIRE Victory: Free Speech at William & Mary," *www.thefireguides.org*, February 2, 2004.

9. FIRE News, "Student Affirmative Action Bake Sales Shut Down Nationwide," *www. thefireguides.org*, December 13, 2003.

10. O'Neil, 22.

11. O'Neil, 21–22.

12. Nat Hentoff, *Living the Bill of Rights* (New York: HarperCollins, 1998), 188–192.

13. Golding, 23.

chapter 5

Abortion
and Public Opinion

S uspicion of public opinion is an old American tradition. Many parts of the U.S Constitution—for example, the indirect selection of the president through an electoral college, the long six-year terms for senators, and a non-elected judiciary appointed by the president—reflect the fears that popular opinion could fall under the sway of "violent passions." While democratic voices would be heard, the framers worried about frequent and extreme changes of mass opinion. The checks and balances of a divided federal government would, it was hoped, restrain the citizenry.

In recent years, political scientists have come to more positive conclusions about public opinion. In *The Rational Public,* their study of public policy preferences over the last fifty years, Benjamin Page and Robert Shapiro conclude that Americans' opinions about policy are generally quite stable. Not only do the policy choices of the public seldom change, they argue, but these opinions are also generally coherent, consistent, and sensible. In sorting through data from hundreds of polls, the authors conclude that when public opinion does change, it does so in incremental and predictable ways. Accordingly, government policies can, should, and usually do rest on the preferences of ordinary citizens.[1]

The following case shows that public opinion is not something produced only by political leaders, nor are people's opinions completely detached from the political process. Attitudes toward abortion shifted in the 1960s, paralleling the social revolution toward women and sexual behavior that occurred at the time. In the face of attempts by political leaders to manipulate and change it, public opinion on abortion has remained remarkably stable since then. This acceptance of legal abortion has been restrained at times by changes in government policies and the framing of the issue by groups trying to sway public opinion. But while these policies affect public preferences, it is more to the point that government policies sooner or later have to adapt to the public that they seek to represent. Public opinion set the boundaries, and the politics of abortion has played out within these broadly accepted borders over the last thirty years.

Thanks to Professor Clyde Wilcox for reading an early draft of this chapter.

concepts highlighted

1. Since the 1970s, a **moderate, stable majority opinion** has existed on abortion. Intensely committed groups on both sides of the abortion issue have attempted to influence public opinion and government policies. In what situations is there a great deal of stability in public opinion on abortion? In what situations do these majorities narrow? Find examples where the wording of poll questions seems to put public opinion on different sides of the abortion debate.

2. The **government's role in shaping public opinion** is both complicated and incomplete. Find examples where government has responded to public opinion on abortion by structuring legislation or court opinions that reflect major changes in popular opinion. Give other examples where government has attempted to lead opinion by shaping public policies. Either way, does government seem to be out of line with popular opinion on abortion for very long?

3. The cultural earthquake of the sixties, not the government, was key in **forming political opinion** on abortion. How did the values shift of that period—women's liberation and "the culture of freedom"—apply to this issue? How did pro-abortion groups organize to turn a favorable change in opinion into new laws and government policies?

4. Look for examples of anti-abortion interest groups **marketing political issues**. How did they position themselves on the majority side of issues like partial-birth abortion and parental consent for minors that would advance their overall agenda of preventing abortion? Did this marketing have a lasting impact on majority public opinion?

Yet another battle in the abortion wars broke out in the fall of 2003. On November 5 President George W. Bush signed a law banning a late-term abortion procedure he called partial-birth. One anti-abortion leader declared, "Today is a monumental day for the sanctity of human life." On the other side, an abortion rights group saw dark plotting by the bill's sponsors "to take away entirely the right to personal privacy and a woman's right to choose."[2] The day did seem significant. For the first time in thirty years, since the Supreme Court allowed women to terminate their pregnancies in the 1973 *Roe v. Wade* decision, a specific abortion procedure was prohibited. The law had passed both houses overwhelmingly. In the Senate the vote was 64 to 34, which included the support of seventeen Democratic senators, many of them strong advocates of abortion rights.

For committed opponents of abortion, the partial-birth decision was a "teaching moment," part of a gradual strategy to turn public opinion against *Roe v. Wade*. These opponents believed that their movement was succeeding: Congress had enacted laws limiting federal financing for abortions, forty-four states had requirements for parental consent, and there appeared to be widespread approval for restrictions on abortion.

Yet this apparent victory for abortion foes may have been deceptive. There had never been much public support for allowing abortions late in a pregnancy. Most people viewed terminating a pregnancy beyond eighteen weeks as sufficiently distasteful to be criminalized. Even among supporters there was considerable debate on the impact of the ban. Many saw it as "purely symbolic" rather than a clear victory for anti-abortion activists. The partial-birth procedure involved fewer than one-fifth of 1 percent of all abortions. When brought before several federal judges, enforcement of the law was halted because it did not provide for any protection where the mother's health was at stake. Legal experts thought the Supreme Court would overturn the law as inconsistent with *Roe*. One analyst remarked about the politicians' calculations, "You make the constituency happy by signing it into law, and then the big bad courts torpedo it, and nobody's talking about it." The president of the pro-life American Life League complained about her Republican allies' support of this ban: "It was the least they could possibly get away with in order to receive the pro-life vote."[3]

Despite the new law, the anti-abortion forces in this "Clash of Absolutes" had not achieved a clear victory. In fact, both sides faced a similar dilemma: *Public opinion on abortion has remained the same for the last thirty years.* Beneath the sound and fury of political battles and the millions of dollars spent by intensely warring groups to market their side of the issue so that it would gain a favorable public response—such as the graphic descriptions of the partial-birth procedure—popular opinion remained unmoved.

The Stability of Public Opinion on Abortion

The consistency of public opinion seems clear. A defining study of polls on abortion concluded that "public opinion on abortion has been remarkably stable" since the *Roe v. Wade* decision of 1973.[4] The Gallup poll shows little change since 1975. In that year roughly the same percentages of people surveyed said abortion should be legal under any circumstances as said it should always be illegal—21 percent versus 22 percent. Fifty-four percent stood firmly in the middle, wanting abortion legal only under certain circumstances. These positions varied only slightly over the next three decades: In January 2003, 24 percent of those polled believed abortion should always be legal, 18 percent believed it should always be illegal, and 57 percent thought abortion should be legal in some circumstances.[5] In his recent argument against "the myth of a polarized America," Morris P. Fiorina concluded that nearly two-thirds of Americans supported *Roe v. Wade*. Other pollsters' findings are similar.[6]

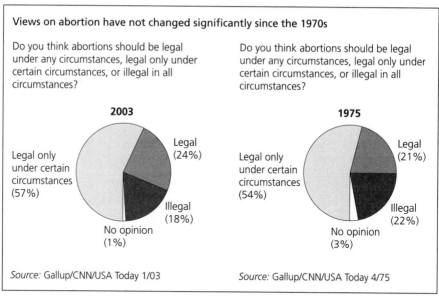

Views on abortion have not changed significantly since the 1970s

Do you think abortions should be legal under any circumstances, legal only under certain circumstances, or illegal in all circumstances?

2003

Legal only under certain circumstances (57%)

Legal (24%)

Illegal (18%)

No opinion (1%)

Source: Gallup/CNN/USA Today 1/03

Do you think abortions should be legal under any circumstances, legal only under certain circumstances, or illegal in all circumstances?

1975

Legal only under certain circumstances (54%)

Legal (21%)

Illegal (22%)

No opinion (3%)

Source: Gallup/CNN/USA Today 4/75

Figure 5.1 Views on Abortion, 1975 and 2003
Copyright © 2004 Public Agenda

Saying that public opinion on abortion is stable doesn't mean it is one-dimensional. As Everett Carll Ladd and Karlyn H. Bowman put it, "Some questions pull people in one direction, others draw them in another. Opinion is not only clear; it is also complex."

The majority of Americans hold opinions somewhere between unlimited access and total prohibition of abortion. American attitudes are stable because they lie between two important, if seemingly contrasting beliefs—one that abortion is murder, the other that only a woman can make the decision to terminate her pregnancy. In a *Los Angeles Times* poll in 2000, 60 percent considered abortion murder. Yet in the same poll, over 70 percent agreed with the statement "No matter how I feel about abortion, I believe it is a decision that has to be made by a woman and her doctor." Americans endorse both the sanctity of life and the importance of individual choice. These positions have been "rock solid" for the last quarter century.[7]

Oddly enough, both pro-life and pro-choice groups can claim majority support for their positions. Activists from the pro-choice camp correctly point out that a majority of Americans disapproves of a ban on abortion. Pro-life groups contend that a majority does not favor abortion on demand—also correct. In fact, most Americans hold an in-between position—legal abortion in the first trimester, but with limits on its use.[8] Nearly two-thirds say abortion should be generally legal in the first three months, but large majorities say it should be illegal in the second and third trimesters. A CNN/USA Today/Gallup poll in October 2003 on the late pregnancy partial-birth abortion found that 68 percent favored making it illegal.[9]

Caught between clashing absolutes, Americans are "situationalists." The situations where the public justifies and opposes abortion are clearly separated. Huge majorities (nine out of ten) support it when the woman's own health is endangered by the pregnancy. Equal support is found where there is a strong chance of a serious defect in the baby or where the pregnancy is the result of rape. In other words, public opinion wants abortion legal in these three *traumatic* circumstances—when the health of the mother is at stake, where there is a defective fetus, or in cases of rape. But in *elective* circumstances, these majorities disappear. The public is conflicted about legal abortion when the family has a very low income and cannot afford any more children; when the woman is married but does not want any more children; or when a woman is not married and does not want to marry the man. In these cases—poverty, unwanted pregnancy, unmarried mother—a narrow majority opposes allowing an abortion.[10]

Attitudes toward abortion are related to demographic factors including age, education, and religion, as well as general political leanings. Education is the strongest predictor of positions on abortion. Opposition to abortion is lowest among college graduates and highest among high school dropouts. Those with the best jobs and the highest incomes are more likely to support legal abortion. Younger voters are more liberal about abortion policy than are older voters. With regard to religion, Protestants and Catholics actually look alike in their attitudes. More difference is found in *how* religious people are: those who rarely attend church—whether Protestant or Catholic—are more likely to support abortion. Democrats support abortion at twice the rate of Republicans. However, in exit polls taken in recent presidential elections, less than a majority of Democrats favored unlimited abortion.[11]

The Historic Change in Public Opinion

These views reflect broad historic trends. They developed as part of the country's changing approach to social issues, including sexual morality, the roles of women in society, and the importance of childbearing and families. These trends were all closely linked with a national upheaval popularly known as "The Sixties."

The Gallup poll did not even ask about abortion until 1962, both because it was not an issue and because it was too sensitive to discuss. In that year the media began to cover the plight of an Arizona woman, Sherri Finkbine, who went to Sweden for an abortion. During her pregnancy, she had taken the drug thalidomide, which was later found to cause birth defects, and she feared having a deformed baby. Because her life wasn't endangered by the pregnancy, she couldn't get an abortion legally in her state. At the time, only a bare majority of Americans approved of what she did.

Prior to the 1960s, the idea of abortion, indeed the very word, was considered so unpleasant that the issue was excluded from the nation's political agenda. When public debate over abortion emerged, every state had criminal laws forbidding the intentional termination of pregnancy, with the single exception being to save the life of the mother. These statutes often dated back to the nineteenth century. For example, Connecticut law written in 1821 made aborting a fetus a criminal offense after its "quickening," or the first evidence of movement inside the womb. By the 1960s, most states had laws on the books making abortion a crime.

It was because of a larger shift in cultural values in the late 1960s, including the growth of feminism, that abortion surfaced as an issue for public discussion. The "boundary-breaking demands for personal freedom" of the decade brought the issue of abortion forcibly to the American public's attention. As part of this "culture of freedom," emphasis was put on individuals' rights to make choices that affected their lives, and this meant questioning the limits of public regulation on private conduct. The feminist movement of the sixties applied that freedom to women's control over their own bodies. Abortion was identified with this individual freedom.[12] The "culture of freedom" energized a social and sexual revolution in thinking. Liberal attitudes toward abortion were spreading on college campuses and among those with few ties to organized religion. Ideas about women's changing role in society were widely discussed, paralleled by growing public support for the women's movement. Federalism played a role as throughout the sixties, states began to pass laws permitting abortion. These early laws usually followed a "model statute" that allowed for abortions in cases of rape, incest, or medical necessity. Other states went further to legalize abortions performed on any medical grounds. As some states passed laws allowing abortions, women traveled to those states to end unwanted pregnancies, which intensified the national debate carried in the media.

College-educated young people were turning away from their parents' beliefs and embracing new ideas about personal freedom. By 1972, most college graduates favored abortion on demand compared to only one-third of people without high school degrees. Among people saying religion should have *less* of a role in national life, three out of five supported abortion. Among those who believed religion should have a *greater* role, only one in five backed abortion on demand. Catholics demonstrated an especially striking change. In 1962, one-third of Catholics supported Sherri Finkbine's right to an abortion. Since 1972, surveys have shown that 77 percent of Catholics support abortion where there is a strong chance of a serious birth defect.

Government, Groups, and Public Opinion

To say that the stability of public opinion on abortion reflects long-term cultural shifts is not to say that opinion is unchanging. Both government and activist groups have attempted to influence opinion, and at times have succeeded, at least around the edges. Government—legislatures, courts, and presidents—has announced policies and shown leadership on the issue. Organized interests, both for and against abortion, have pushed specific policies that they felt would gain public support. By presenting their views on this complex issue in a favorable framework, such groups have moved the debate for limited periods. Yet all these political groups' shaping of public opinion had neither the impact nor the durability of the broad social changes brought by the sixties. For policies on abortion to work, they had to operate within the existing boundaries.

In 1973, the Supreme Court, in *Roe v. Wade,* legalized abortion in the first three months of a pregnancy. Not only did this decision reflect the change in public opinion since the mid-1960s, but it helped move that opinion further. One pollster concluded: "That jump in support after the court decision was sharper than in any other two-year period of polling; it signified a switch in position for some ten million adult Americans."[13] The increased support remained high into the 1980s and may have reflected the Supreme Court's prestige as an authority interpreting the Constitution. It may also speak to the polarized nature of the case: forcing people to choose whether abortion should or should not be allowed.

Pro-abortion groups had helped change public opinion leading up to the *Roe* decision. Activists had pushed for reforming state laws based on an argument of personal liberty. Civil liberties and women's groups identified abortion as a constitutionally protected right of privacy. They were aided by organized medicine, notably the American Medical Association. In 1967, the AMA had passed a resolution supporting liberalized abortion laws, although theirs was an argument for professional control, rather than personal freedom. The physicians framed the issue as a medical one, to be decided by a woman and her doctor, in which political and legal factors had no place.

The themes of professional autonomy and personal privacy were joined by an argument of social policy. Groups concerned with overpopulation, such as Planned Parenthood, had been focused on birth control policies and had historically opposed abortion. Pressured by more radical groups, like Zero Population Growth, Planned Parenthood signed on to the pro-abortion coalition. Bolstered by civil liberties allies and supporters in organized medicine, Planned Parenthood became an advocate for removing legal barriers to abortion as one method for dealing with the "population bomb."[14]

Abortion Opponents

The modifying of abortion laws faced stern opposition. "Right to Life" committees were formed in many states to prevent further changes in the laws and to encourage stricter bans. The Catholic Church was the most persistent opponent, although it was joined by fundamentalist Christians and Orthodox Jews. The rise of conservatism in the 1980s, including President Reagan's frequent speeches against abortion, may have led to a slight decline in public support.

Instead of trying to directly overturn the reformed abortion laws—and put themselves outside the boundaries of public opinion—opponents marketed their anti-abortion position around more popular issues. During the 1980s the most common debate about abortion centered on parental notification and consent for minors seeking abortions. By focusing the discussion around parental notification, public support for this limit on abortion was assured. Parents' consent for minors' abortions received over 80 percent support in opinion polls. Since this concern was uppermost in the public's mind, it too may have reduced overall support for abortion.[15]

The Supreme Court's July 3, 1989, ruling in *Webster v. Reproductive Health Services* allowed states to put some restrictions on abortion, which returned the issue to various state legislatures and focused debate on limiting women's access. The initial reaction to the decision was to increase membership and donations to groups on both sides of the abortion issue. Pro-abortion groups, feeling more threatened by these government restraints, initially saw a dramatic increase in their support.[16]

In the 1990s, opponents of abortion focused on a late-term procedure they called partial-birth abortion, hoping Congress would lead public opinion. On the floor of the Senate, opponents argued with graphic charts and drawings that partial-birth abortion was no abstract clash of rights; this was infanticide. With the shift in public debate to a late-term procedure, the overall support for abortion dipped. The framing of the policy debate by political leaders once again caused a minor change in the poll numbers, at least for a while.[17] As a Republican senator said, "With partial-birth abortion, you can't miss the baby."

Bills banning partial-birth abortion were passed twice by Congress after the Republicans gained control in 1994, but were vetoed by President Clinton. Upon his veto of April 1996 President Clinton brought five women who had had the procedure to the White House to speak tearfully of their agonizing decisions in dealing with the disorders threatening them and their fetuses. When President Bush signed similar legislation seven and a half years later he declared, "Today, at last, the American people and our government have confronted the violence and come to the defense of the innocent child." The struggle for public opinion continues.[18]

Pro-choice and pro-life demonstrators line up on either side of the abortion issue on the anniversary of the *Roe v. Wade* decision.
© David Bacon/The Image Works

Conclusion

Over twenty years ago, political scientist Austin Sarat concluded, "In the final analysis, the shifting fortunes of abortion politics cannot be attributed to the actions of any group or institution, but rather to the rhythms of the larger culture."[19] The public's acceptance of legal abortion three decades ago was a result of a vast social change in attitudes labeled "the Sixties." A deep belief in personal freedom, decreasing support for religion, a better-educated youth, and a growing women's movement all led to this acceptance. Professional and interest groups, state governments, and then the Supreme Court both supported this trend and followed it. Since then, opposition groups and elected officials have tried to restrict abortion by marketing their issues around policies like parental consent and partial-birth to take advantage of the boundaries of its public support. Nor can one ignore the impact of intimidation, including the bombing of clinics, in limiting women's willingness to seek abortions.[20]

But underlying the headlines, the polarized debates, and seeming shifts in political sentiment is a public opinion that has remained quite stable over a long period of time. The conclusions of the American public represent a balanced exercise of national judgment. They show the public reacting to available information and reaching moderate opinions as to how abortion should be permitted and limited. These conclusions, of course, may change. Some scholars think that a recent rise in conservative opinion undermining support for abortion may be the result of new ultrasound technology that produces pictures of early-stage fetuses and encourages a belief, especially among young women, that life begins at conception. Others conclude differently—that a younger generation constantly replaces an older one, bringing higher education rates, a larger urban population, and more exposure to modernizing ideas, leading to a long-term liberalizing of public opinion on issues like abortion.[21]

For our conclusion, we are willing to suspend our powers of prediction and agree with Drs. Page and Shapiro: "What the public thinks about a given policy now is a very strong indicator of what it will think later."[22] This stable body of opinion sets boundaries around the political choices available to policymakers. To outlaw abortions now wouldn't be easy. It would require more than a Supreme Court decision, a bill by Congress, or even a Constitutional amendment. It would need a revolution in thinking similar to the one that began in the 1960s.

Notes

1. Benjamin I. Page and Robert Y. Shapiro, *The Rational Public* (Chicago: University of Chicago Press, 1992).
2. Sheryl Gay Stolberg, "The War Over Abortion Moves to a Smaller Stage," *New York Times*, October 26, 2003, 4.
3. Stolberg, "The War Over Abortion."
4. Everett Carll Ladd and Karlyn H. Bowman, *Public Opinion About Abortion*, 2nd ed. (Washington, DC: AEI Press, 1999), 1.
5. As cited by Public Agenda Online at *www.publicagendaonline.com*.
6. See Morris P. Fiorina et al., *Culture War? The Myth of a Polarized America* (New York: Pearson, 2005), Chapter 4, "A Closer Look at Abortion."
7. Clyde Wilcox and Barbara Norrander, "Of Moods and Morals: The Dynamics of Opinion on Abortion and Gay Rights," in Clyde Wilcox and Barbara Norrander, *Understanding Public Opinion*, 2nd ed. (Washington, DC: Congressional Quarterly Press, 2001).
8. Elizabeth Adell Cook, Ted G. Jelen, and Clyde Wilcox, *Between Two Absolutes: Public Opinion and the Politics of Abortion* (Boulder, CO: Westview Press, 1992), 37.
9. See *PollingReport.com/abortion.htm*, p. 1.
10. Cook, Jelen, and Wilcox, 36.
11. Ladd and Bowman, 15.
12. See Austin Sarat, "Abortion and the Courts: Uncertain Boundaries of Law and Politics," in Allan P. Sindler, ed., *American Politics and Public Policy: Seven Case Studies* (Washington, DC: Congressional Quarterly Press, 1982), 124–125.

13. Barry Sussman, *What Americans Really Think* (New York: Pantheon, 1988), 192–199.

14. Sarat, 126–128.

15. Clyde Wilcox and Julia Riches, "Pills in the Public's Mind: RU 48 and the Framing of the Abortion Issue," *Women and Politics* 24, no. 3 (2002): 68–69.

16. Carol Matlock, "Mobilizing for the Abortion War," *National Journal*, July 15, 1989, 1814–1815.

17. Wilcox and Riches, 68.

18. Robin Toner, "For GOP, It's a Moment," *New York Times*, November 6, 2003, A16.

19. Sarat, 127.

20. See Patricia Baird-Windle and Eleanor J. Bader, *Targets of Hatred: Anti-Abortion Terrorism* (New York: Palgrave, 2001).

21. The first opinion is from Wilcox and Norrander; the second is from Robert Erikson and Kent Tedin, *American Public Opinion*, 5th ed. (Needham Heights, MA: Allyn and Bacon, 1995), 115–116.

22. Page and Shapiro, 385.

chapter 6

Redistricting Reelection

A Campaign Manager's View

Elections can be exciting. They can be bruising battles between articulate rivals over issues of policies and values, experience and character. Even their frequent nastiness shows the vigor and importance of an open political marketplace. Elections are the method by which a democracy chooses its leaders in a public contest for popular support. At least, they're supposed to be.

From the viewpoint of those playing the election game, the goal is to win a powerful position. Generally, the person already in the job has the edge in name recognition, money, experience, and a paid office staff. In races for the House of Representatives, these incumbents have even greater advantages because they are able to change the playing field—quite literally. The redrawing of congressional districts after each decade's census offers the political party controlling state government the chance to maximize their favorable districts, while minimizing those of their opponents. In 2002 this advantage produced a House where only four challengers defeated incumbents, the fewest in history. Fewer than 30 out of 435 House seats were considered in play in the 2004 elections, meaning a challenger had more than a prayer of winning; five of these challengers actually won in 2004. The results are "choiceless elections" that rubberstamp the nominee of the party that drew the legislative boundaries.[1]

The following interview with a young campaign manager reflects this reality. David "Duke" Hernandez is a twenty-seven-year-old Californian, a former high school wrestler only a few pounds over his fighting weight. Although he sometimes drops phrases from the barrio, he is the son of two teachers and an honors college graduate. In 2002 he managed the reelection campaign of a California congressman we will call Dick Hayes. The story is Duke's, but all names and identifying facts have been changed to allow us to hear an insider's frank views of what happens in most of the 98 percent of the races where House incumbents won reelection last time for "The People's House."

concepts highlighted

1. The **advantages of incumbency** come through clearly in this campaign manager's story. Of those mentioned, which are the most important—redistricting, experience in office, public recognition, fundraising, professional consultants, or congressional staff—in explaining the high rates of incumbent reelections? How can a challenger overcome these incumbent advantages?

2. The campaign spends considerable effort **manipulating the electoral process**. Redistricting is an important part of that process. How does the campaign influence the size and composition of the electorate? Would redistricting tend to produce less moderate, more partisan Congress members dependent on core supporters, as some have charged? How does the campaign staff encourage supporters to vote, while discouraging its opponents from voting?

3. How important is **fundraising** in the campaign? Do the people contributing money have a major influence over the candidate? Could their impact be out of sight of the young campaign manager? Would any campaign finance reform, such as lower limits, change how the campaign raises money or the influence of money in elections? Would it make campaigning more difficult for incumbents or challengers?

4. Some one-third of eligible voters turn out for congressional elections. Is **voter participation** encouraged by the strategy and tactics of this campaign? Does the campaign manager want a large number of new voters to participate on Election Day? Does his realistic description of the inside workings of a campaign encourage you to vote?

5. Despite the flaws in campaigns and elections, are there still **benefits flowing from elections**? How does even a reelection to a "safe seat" pressure a member of Congress to leave the bright lights of Washington to meet constituents, talk with interest groups, and raise money? How do elected officials benefit from a campaign? How do voters?

Note: Although this case is in the campaign manager's own words, author comments have been inserted throughout in italics.

The first thing to understand about being a campaign manager for a congressman's reelection is that it isn't very intellectually demanding. It's pretty mechanical. Most of the creative work was done before I arrived on the scene. The redistricting that was done after the 2000 census made all the difference. You could call it an "incumbent-protection racket."[2]

The Redistricting Racket

After the 2000 census, California legislators deliberately drew congressional district boundaries in ways designed to eliminate competition. . . .
Their redistricting scheme took away the voters' power to choose.

Thomas E. Patterson, *The Vanishing Voter*

California's 56th District, which Congressman Dick Hayes represents, has usually been marginally Democratic. Hayes first won it in 1996 when it was an open seat, against a moderate Republican woman. He won by a couple of points, outspending her by a lot; a right-wing Libertarian candidate took 5,000 votes, which was more than our margin of victory. 1998 was pretty much a repeat of the first race, with Dick increasing his margin a bit in a lower-turnout non-presidential election year. Then in 2000 the Republicans targeted the district, figuring that with redistricting coming up, this would be their last chance to win the seat. Despite recruiting a strong candidate and putting money into the race, the GOP lost. With [Al] Gore at the top of the [Democratic] ticket winning 57 percent in California, Hayes won with 52 percent of the vote, which was 3 points over a moderate former congressman. So before the 2000 census, the 56th was Democratic, but only by 2 to 3 percent.

As you know, after the census every state legislature draws up new maps for its congressional districts, which then go to the governor for his approval. The state got one more congressional seat because of population increase. Since in California at the time Democrats controlled the assembly and the governorship, the party was expected to help itself. The party didn't gain as many seats from redistricting as the Republicans did in Texas, because the Democratic incumbents wanted to make sure their own seats were safe. So rather than help the party by moving Democratic voters to Republican districts and make them close races, most California incumbents took care of themselves by adding Dems to their own districts. That's what my congressman did.[3]

The congressman had discussions with a senior staff guy in the state assembly, which I wasn't part of. I heard they ran through the results of some sophisticated computer map programs to figure out how to make the seat safe. Of course, there were a lot of other pols besides Dick interested in the redistricted map. The result was that we cut out an upper-middle-class Republican area and added two Hispanic communities on either end of the district that were overwhelmingly Democratic. Overnight our district went from a 2 to 3 percent Democratic margin to a pretty secure 12 percent Democratic advantage in registered voters.

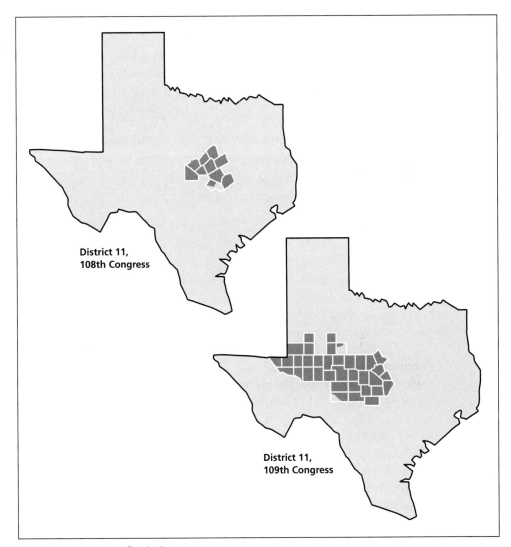

Figure 6.1 Texas Redistricting

The redistricting also managed to pack the Republicans into one neighboring district. So instead of having two marginally Republican districts bordering us, we ended up with one solidly Republican district and one where a Democrat could win. (One Republican incumbent was forced to run in this new district and lost to a Democrat in 2002.) Meanwhile we doubled our Hispanic population so that it became 30 percent of the district. Hayes actually would have preferred another upscale liberal Democratic area, but lost out to a neighboring Democratic congresswoman who had more seniority and more clout in the [State] Assembly. The congressman now worries about some young Hispanic activist organizing the area and running against him in a future primary.

The bottom line for us was that the 56th became a safe Democratic district. Our consultant predicted that 175,000 voters would go to the polls. But whether turnout was high or low would not make any difference in the race. Hayes was likely to exceed the 60 percent standard for a safe seat. The consultant concluded, "I anticipate an uneventful, easy win [for Hayes] this year, and uncomplicated reelections for years to come."

Fill 'er Up

Beyond redistricting, a major advantage that congressional incumbents bring to their races is fundraising. Having substantial money in the bank long before the campaign begins discourages opponents. Incumbents depend on a network of contributors who want to help for personal and policy reasons. In elections below the level of well-publicized presidential campaigns, the use of mail or the Internet for fundraising is less important than mobilizing this personal network.

Fundraising for the campaign had been completed by June '01. This meant that a year before the election started, we had a million dollars in the bank. It was a way of looking strong and keeping any pols looking for a job out of the race. Most of the fundraising was done by a hired consultant, but I [observed] what she was doing.

Basically, after his years in office Dick had a network of rich friends. Some of them were connected to the energy and environment subcommittee where he was the ranking Democrat, but most were just people who liked him. There were not a lot of deals going on when the congressman called. Nobody would ever say, "I like his bill, here's the money." Most had started giving money so long ago they just kept doing it. Many liked to tell their friends that the congressman had called them. And as the fundraising consultant told me repeatedly, "People give money to people not causes."

Most of the money was raised at fundraisers put on by the members of Dick's campaign finance committee, his wealthy buddies. Each would commit to raising, say, $50,000 and then would invite 200 friends and business associates to a party at their house for $1,000 each—the legal maximum [per election] at the time. So there's an energy attorney who knows Dick, he teams up with some Hollywood agents who like to keep their hands in politics, they put together the lists, and you've got your event. Rich people don't really care about the events; they'll give the money whether they come or not. They do want to be asked. The only problem this time was convincing them that Dick needed the money for his safe seat. Our consultant liked these parties. As she said, "The $50,000 parties get you what you need pretty quickly. The $10,000 events take forever."

We raised about half the money we needed from these events. A third of the money came from the Dinner Honoring Congressman Hayes, which is held every other year. We raise about $350,000 with about 700 people attending at $500 a ticket. Last time we got Al Gore as the guest speaker. The hotel and the meal cost us a pretty steep $60 a person. One of the tricks of fundraising is to keep your costs down. The rest of the money, say $150,000, comes from DC events—some breakfasts and receptions given by PACs [political action committees]. Also the other members of Congress, especially the leadership, will help out by giving fundraisers for us.

The congressman was pretty good about making the calls. A lot of members have to have their arms twisted to ask people for money. Our fundraising consultant would put together lists of donors, and then Dick would check off the ones he would call. We didn't use either the Internet or mail to raise money. Our consultant thought these only worked in presidential campaigns where you could get ideological giving.

One thing that definitely didn't work was fundraising in the district. Very few of the people we were raising money from lived in the district. We had some "Pancake events" there at $50 a ticket, but that was pretty much for show.

Getting Staffed

An experienced staff dedicated to its congressman is another ingredient in a successful election. Young people—hard working, loyal, and inexpensive—comprise most election campaigns. This advantage is somewhat limited by the law forbidding the use of office staff (who are government employees) from directly aiding a campaign.

So after we have the redistricting down and the money in the bank, I walk in. I had started as a volunteer on Hayes's 2000 campaign. I did everything—driver, scheduling, advance on events, and all-around "go-fer." Speaking Spanish helped in the projects, and I worked fourteen-hour days helping out on the phone banks and doing everything anybody asked me to. After the campaign was over, the congressman asked me to join his district office as a field representative. Since I was just out of college, I jumped at the chance. It was a good job, paid about $35,000, and I got to help a lot of compadres with things like Social Security disability checks and veterans benefits. I organized high-visibility events for the congressman and worked for community groups trying to keep the district's navy shipyard open. A lot of my work was keeping in touch with the unions and neighborhood groups to make sure they had the congressman's ear.

I think Dick is an incredibly effective congressman. He focuses on a couple of issues—the environment and alternative energy development—got pilot projects into the district, and increased spending for national programs as well. He also plays by the rules. He'll stand up to local groups when they make demands that he just can't support. Dick is so bright and articulate that he's tough to argue with.

He can be difficult to work for. Staff turnover is high. I remember him hiring a woman who had an MBA and campaign experience to be his AA [Administrative Assistant], which is the top staff job. One evening they worked late, and Dick asked her to drop him off at a dinner reception. When they got there, he told her that he would just be a minute and asked if she could wait for him. He was inside for over an hour while the AA waited in the car. She quit the next day.

We get on pretty well. He reminds me of my dad, strict but pretty fair once you show you'll stand up for yourself. We talk a lot about baseball. We both like the Padres.

In March 2002 he asked me to run the campaign. In the past Dick had hired a professional campaign manager. Now he asked me because he trusted me, and because I was cheap. Because of federal laws, there is supposed to be a firewall between congressional staff and the campaign—federal employees are not allowed to do campaign work. This meant that for the first two months I went half time, working from my home for two days a week and in the district office for three days.

Of course, this was easier said than done. I was supposed to use my own computer and my own phone for campaign matters, but things got sloppy. I'd be talking to the congressman from the district office and he'd ask "what about that fundraising letter?" or about a campaign event. Most of the messages for the campaign came out of speeches written in Washington, and we would design events in the district around themes of the campaign. While he got trips to the district paid for as a congressman, he couldn't go into the new parts of the district unless the event was charged against campaign funds. So we held events in bordering areas. That way we could make it official business.

In June I went full time, and my first job was to set up the campaign office. We could have gotten by without one, but Dick wanted to make sure that the people who had worked in his previous campaigns kept involved in this one. So the campaign office, maybe the campaign itself, was essentially aimed at holding on to supporters. We shared the office— a storefront—with the local assemblyperson. The carpenters' union put up the dividing wall for us—an in-kind contribution. We had twenty phone lines put in, a fax, a copier, and rented computers. Dick hired a field director/volunteer coordinator. She was twenty-four and had been an intern in the office. The office also served as the local headquarters for the Democratic party.[4]

Calls, Contacts, and the Candidate

Even a noncompetitive election becomes an opportunity for an incumbent to (re)connect with constituents. Whatever the strength of the congressman's ties with his district, campaign events give him publicity and a chance to address local concerns. A campaign energizes supporters and allows important interest groups to gain "face time" with the member.

Much of what I did revolved around phoning voters. The phone banks were used most evenings between 5 and 8 p.m. to call high-propensity voters (people who voted in at least half of the previous six elections) who leaned Democratic. We excluded diehard Democrats and Republicans, figuring that neither would change their minds. We made about 1,500 calls a night. Our callers, following a phone script, asked if the potential voters were supporting Hayes, and then recorded the yes's and maybe's. If they answered no, we ended the call. The others got a thank you postcard signed by the congressman, adding that if they had any questions to please call headquarters.

My days consisted of making sure the data from the previous night's phoning was entered into the computer and organizing the phone bank for the next night. My biggest problem was to recruit volunteers to make calls for a noncompetitive race. I tried to get targeted groups to commit to one night. So the local teachers union might turn out twenty members to come in on a Tuesday night. The next night might be an environmental call night for Green groups; another might be held for local elected officials. We got the local Service Employees Union to make calls in Spanish one evening. We e-mailed or faxed the "Campaign Weekly" newsletter to 1,200 core supporters where we publicized their efforts and gave them credit for their work.

During the day there would be a half-dozen people in the office. They might be interns from the local high school who were getting class credit, or blue hairs [seniors] putting stamps on envelopes, or a guy coming out

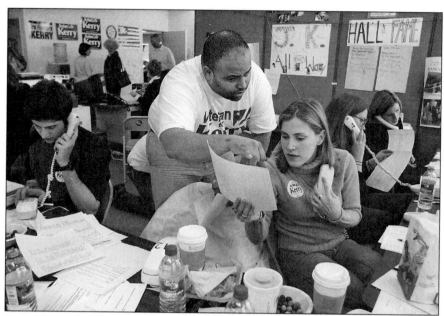

Campaigns often make up in volunteer energy what they lack in professional organization.
© Lou Dematteis/Reuters/Corbis

of a divorce or an unemployed techie with time on his hands. Often the volunteers seemed to be people with something missing in their lives.

Our best help came from organized groups that were clear about what they wanted. We'd have a couple union guys—usually Longshoremen or Teamsters—assigned to take care of us, and they would make sure we got the help we needed. They would drive the congressman around, walk the district with him, make phone calls, and help set up events. They followed legislation affecting the unions and used their access with Dick to talk to him about, say, port security or pension bills in Congress. They were happy about the access they got, even if they were not always happy with the results of the discussions. But they got "face time" with Dick that they would never have gotten in Washington. And when they went to DC, they'd see the congressman, not some junior staff person.[5]

Seeing the candidate in the [home] district wasn't that easy either. Dick only showed up in the district a couple of times a month. While he wanted local visibility for the folks back home, Dick has a pretty bad case of "Potomac Fever." Most of the time he'd rather be in DC. His kids were in school there, his wife had gotten to like Georgetown tea parties, and he found mixing with the "movers and shakers" a lot more exciting than kissing babies in our farmers' market on a Saturday morning.

Dick had gotten his start in politics as a political appointee in the Carter administration. When he went back into the family business afterward, it just wasn't as exciting. So he took some of his family's money—and there was a lot left over—to use in his run for Congress. He ran one sacrificial race where he lost but learned, and then put it together to win in 1996. Dick was a policy-wonk; he certainly did his homework on the issues I dealt with. He was also a tough-minded liberal who did right by the people in his district. He just didn't want to spend much time with them.[6]

Consultants and Mail

Modern campaigns need professionals. Experts in fundraising, mail, voter contact, and campaign strategy are sought after and highly rewarded. That is not to say that campaigning has become a science. It involves trial and error, judgment calls, and a fair amount of wasted time and money.

The campaign consultants were a group I'll call DNA Associates, who were basically a direct mail firm. They had a national reputation and were already doing a dozen races. During the interviews, I wasn't sure who was auditioning who; Dick thought we were lucky to get them. They were basically looking either for high-profile races to aid in future marketing or for easy money. At the $35,000 a month they cost, we fell in the latter category. They were pros, and they saw the rest of us as amateurs. We were a business for them—no more, no less.

They did our direct mail and supplied lists of names and numbers for our phone banks. We had a weekly conference call with their top guy and ran everything by him—brochures, messages, and strategy. Although the mailings were taken from stuff written by the congressional staff, DNA went over the message. They targeted the new areas of the district [the ones added on by redistricting], and included a letter by Cruz Bustamante, California's lieutenant governor and the state's highest-ranking Hispanic official. Our messages were traditional Democratic ones: health care, education, and jobs.

Mail ended up being the biggest item in the budget, taking about one-third of a budget that was just under a million dollars. We did eleven mail pieces, four of them going to swing [undecided] voters. We did an environmental piece, a woman piece, and a security/terrorist mailing. We did a mailing to Republicans that had endorsements of Dick by Republican officials. Since education was Dick's big issue, we sent a pamphlet on education that included a note from the president praising Dick's work on the No Child Left Behind education reform. We sent a mailing to all households with Latino last names with Hispanic leaders' endorsements.

We sent a lot of mail into the two new areas in the district. To introduce the new voters to the congressman, we mailed Dick's bio to all registered voters in these new parts of the district. Dick wanted a strong showing there in order to discourage some Lefty Latino from running against him in a future primary. We tried going door-to-door to register people to vote. (In one of the new areas, Alberta, there were 4,280 registered voters out of 23,180 people.) But it didn't go well. Citizenship was an issue. We found most of the people living there were illegals [illegal immigrants] who couldn't have registered if they wanted to. Families were crowded into a couple of rooms, and most wouldn't talk to a stranger. We put door hangers [brochures] on their doorknobs and left. We pulled the plug on the project after a week.[7]

We spent $50,000 on our field operations. After the fiasco in the new areas, most of the remaining money went into the coordinated campaign of the party. This was the effort by the party to put field [organizers] and mail behind all the Democrats who were running in the area for local, state, and federal offices. Dick ended up giving $150,000 from his campaign funds to other Democrats who were running. He did this through his leadership PAC, and it went to vulnerable candidates as well as to young Latino candidates that Dick wanted to get close to. The amount was considered inadequate by the party, given the amounts Dick had and that his race wasn't close.

The Opposition and Election Day

An incumbent's campaign is designed to keep a strong opponent from running. In most instances it works. Often opposition party newcomers run as a beginning step for long-term political ambitions. The race follows a predictable route: the incumbent's party members are turned out on Election Day, and the incumbent wins in a manner designed to discourage future opponents from contesting this "safe" seat.

I guess you noticed that I haven't mentioned our opponent. He really wasn't much of a factor. The national Republicans decided that the district wasn't winnable, so they didn't try to recruit a strong candidate to run or direct many bucks into the race. So you ended up with Frank Grimaldi. He was a young attorney, pleasant enough with a few bucks in his pocket that he could put into his campaign. He had some political ambitions and figured getting his name around town in this election couldn't hurt. The only real danger from Frank was the possibility that he would do better than expected and encourage the Republicans to target the race next time.

Frank put up a few signs, did a couple of radio spots, and got some newspaper ink by accusing Dick of being a carpetbagger who had lost touch with the folks in the district. In the one debate that Dick agreed to do, Frank seemed to wilt when confronting the congressman face to face. Dick knew his stuff and, I think, blew Frank away. We spent about $10,000 on opposition research but most of that was spent investigating Dick's own background. He wanted to see what the Republicans could come up with, especially with the family business—lawsuits, union problems, tax issues, that kind of stuff. Frank never really got much traction in the race.

As we neared Election Day, activities accelerated. We called absentee voters who were registered Dems and who hadn't sent in their ballots. We also visited them and left them door hangers to remind them to vote. Our lists weren't perfect. I remember some of our volunteers found Republican signs in the front yards of some of the houses we visited.

Then on the Monday before the election we brought in our volunteers to phone our "yes" universe. We would tell them where their polling station was and what time it opened. And we offered them rides if they needed them. We called all the names in the new areas of the district. On Election Day we got lists of voters who had voted in the morning and called the others to remind them to vote.

I'm not sure how effective the whole campaign was. Even a good campaign probably doesn't influence more than a few percent of the vote. It did keep our own people involved, didn't cost much money, and it reinforced the congressman's identity with the district. We won with a little over 60 percent. That means we are now a safe seat, which was the goal.

In November 2004 the congressman won reelection with 62 percent of the vote. His Republican opponent received 33 percent.

Notes

1. See David J. Garrow, "Running the House," *New York Times Magazine*, November 13, 2002. Also see Steven Hill and Rob Richie, "The Dangers of Perpetual Redistricting," The Center for Voting and Democracy, July 1, 2003; and The Campaign Finance Institute, Press Releases, Washington, DC, November 5, 2004, at *www.cfinst.org*.

2. "How to Rig an Election," *The Economist*, Print Edition, April 25, 2002.

3. An excellent analysis of the unprecedented GOP gerrymandering in Texas a couple of years after the 2000 census can be found in Jeffrey Toobin, "The Great Election Grab," *The New Yorker*, December 8, 2003.

4. A more complete account of organizing a campaign is in Dick Simpson, *Winning Elections: A Handbook of Modern Participatory Politics* (New York: HarperCollins, 1996), Chapter 3.

5. What these organized interests look like to the congressional staff is reflected in Barry M. Casper, *Lost in Washington* (Amherst: University of Massachusetts Press, 2000).

6. Still the best account of how House members see their districts is Richard F. Fenno Jr., *Home Style* (Boston: Little, Brown and Company, 1978).

7. Some other reasons for low voter turnout are discussed in Thomas E. Patterson, *The Vanishing Voter* (New York: Vintage Books, 2003).

chapter 7

Parties and Technology

From Voter Targeting to Internet Blogs

The death of American political parties has frequently been predicted. Noted *Washington Post* reporter David Broder once wrote a book titled *The Party's Over*.[1] (He has since changed his mind.) Still, political scientists point to the rise of candidate-oriented elections where individuals control their own campaigns, to the increased media influence in deciding the outcome of party primaries, and to the reliance on interest groups to channel money into Washington, all as signs of party decline. Paralleling these factors are more voters declaring themselves "independent" of either party, while many others turn their backs on the parties' candidates by deciding not to vote at all.

So what do parties do?

Plenty.

Political parties have become huge fundraising and voter mobilizing operations. Each party—and the candidates operating under the party label—raises as much money as possible. This leads to large sums spent on "party-building" and candidate commercials, on voter targeting and get-out-the-vote (GOTV) campaigns, and, of course, on even more fundraising. The two cases below illustrate these trends. In Colorado, the Republican party effectively used computer technology to help their national and state candidates. In the 2004 Howard Dean campaign, a candidate for the Democratic presidential nomination creatively employed the Internet to mobilize supporters and raise funds. Both cases demonstrate how parties and their candidates can use technology to organize voters for partisan purposes. They also underline why, as Mark Twain said about the rumor of his own demise, the reports of the death of American political parties are, at the least, an exaggeration.[2]

concepts highlighted

1. Political parties have evolved into **service organizations** that provide new campaign techniques to attract electoral support. These techniques include polling, advertising, and public relations, as well as the computer/phone and Internet technologies shown in these cases. Does this mean that the type of people who manage the parties has changed from the days of political bosses? What is the impact of this professionalization?

2. **Voter mobilization**, identifying supporters and getting them to the polls, is now a major task of party and candidate organizations. Does this mobilization make these organizations more democratic? Does it shift power to the voter who must decide to respond to the mail or phone or visit a website? Does Dean's use of the Internet allow for more participation than the Colorado computer/phone techniques? Will either technology affect declining voter turnout?

3. Some political scientists think that the **impact of new political technologies** is to give an advantage to those with wealth and power. Though both political parties employ the same technologies, the Republicans have been most successful in using them in the past. Does the Internet, with its expanding fund-raising and networking abilities, change that impact? Or is the GOP likely to be able to use the Web at least as well as the Democrats?

4. **Candidate-centered campaigns** have been accused of encouraging low turn-out and special-interest influence—by targeting supporters and using a small group of fundraisers. Does the Dean campaign's use of the Web challenge this idea? How did the Internet expand voter participation? Could the Internet also result in narrowing participation?

Back in the spring of 1984, voters in several western states got a phone call—from a computer. A recorded voice announced the following:

"Good evening. This is Reagan-Bush '84 calling you on a special computer that is capable of recording your opinion. Your answers to two short questions are very important and will take less than a minute of your time. Please answer after the tone.

Question No. 1: If the election for president were held today, would you vote for President Reagan or the Democratic candidate? (Tone.)

Question No. 2: There are a number of unregistered voters in your neighborhood. Is there anyone in your household who needs to register? (Tone.)

Thank you and good night."

In some areas the telephoned person replied to the questions by pressing a button on his or her push-button phone—5 to indicate support for the president and 6 to indicate opposition. If 6 was pushed, the computer terminated the interview. Pushing 5, however, opened up the voter to a world of high-tech campaigning, courtesy of the Republican party.[3]

Rocky Mountain Targeting

The phone script above reflected the GOP strategy of voter targeting: identifying unregistered Colorado supporters of the party and its candidates, registering them as Republicans, and encouraging them to vote. Using computers and phone banks, the party targeted these key voters so that later they could be contacted about specific issues or taken to the polls on Election Day. Voter targeting demonstrated the party's effective use of campaign resources to maximize its turnout of supporters.

It was the Republican party's answer to the Democrats' advantages in finding and registering new voters. Nonvoters, concentrated in lower-income and minority groups, overwhelmingly support Democrats, if they vote. For example, in 1988 when Jesse Jackson ran for president, at least nine of every ten new African American voters went Democratic. Volunteers for the Democrats could easily go door to door in a black or poor neighborhood and find a large pool of unregistered voters who leaned toward the party.

This meant that Republican efforts to register new voters couldn't mimic the Democratic approach. Republican supporters were likely to already be voters and tended not to live in self-evident ethnic neighborhoods. One Texas Republican party official put it this way: "The thing about Republican precincts, everybody is registered. I walked my precinct, and 90 percent of the people were registered. We have to be selective." Money and technology shaped the Republican registration strategy.

The "high-tech" campaign in 1984 to locate and register GOP voters created a modern version of the traditional American political machine. Fueled by some $10 million from the party, Republicans aimed to add 2 million voters to the national rolls. In the old days, the parties would gather party loyalists in the back rooms of precincts and hand them "walking-around money" to pass out to citizens to "assist" them in registering and voting. Now the machine operated electronically for the difficult task of identifying solid Republican prospects among the mass of unregistered voters. To find the affluent people who were likely to support Republican candidates and who were not registered, the party's computers ran through a range of lists: mail-order buyers from upscale stores, licensed drivers, homeowners, new utility hookups, and subscribers to the *Wall Street Journal*, to name just a few.

Merging and Purging

Colorado's "political machine" was located in the basement of a Denver bank. Here part-time employees were paid 15 cents above the minimum wage to operate computers costing some $275,000 to reach potential GOP voters. One difference with traditional party hacks came in the instructions given the phone bank operators. "Don't talk politics or issues," Ruth Cullen, who managed the program, told them, "This is a paid phone bank. These people don't know politics. I'd as soon not have them try to speak for the candidates. They are not qualified."

The essence of the Colorado GOP registration strategy was a computerized process known as "merging and purging" of multiple lists. It began with a list of registered Colorado voters (1.2 million of them), purchased from the state for $500. Paid party workers first merged this by computer with a list of all licensed drivers over age eighteen (some 2.2 million). They then "purged" all drivers registered to vote, leaving the names of 800,000 unregistered voters who were licensed drivers.

This list was then cut to 120,000 names by eliminating all unregistered drivers who lived in precincts and zip codes with strong Democratic registration numbers as well as Democratic voting histories. The list of 120,000 was matched with another list containing both names and phone numbers, which had been purchased from a commercial firm. About half of the names produced a match of a phone number and an address—absolutely needed if any calls were to be made.

The resulting 60,000 names were the base from which the phone bank with the computerized message operated. The goal of the phone survey—and the computer-generated questions—was to further reduce the list to 20,000 solid Republican prospects. Following instructions on their computer screens, the phone bank employees called the lists. When they reached the person listed—the prospect—they asked if the person was registered. If the answer was yes, the interview ended since the goal was to register the unregistered.

If the response was no, there was a quick series of questions:

- *Do you intend to vote?*
- *Are you likely to vote for Ronald Reagan?*
- *Would you welcome a letter describing how to register?*

The answers were coded by number: 1 for "Yes," 2 for "No," and 3 for "Maybe." Each time the phone bank operator entered a number, the computer responded with instructions to continue the interview or to say thank you and hang up. For example, if the prospect was opposed to the Republican candidates, or even undecided, the interview was ended then and there.

For those 20,000 making the final cut, the computer automatically generated a letter from the Colorado state GOP chairman: "I was so glad when you told one of our Republican workers that you wanted to vote." The letter gave the prospect the address of the nearest county clerk where they could register.

The names were then sent to their local county Republican executive committee, where someone was assigned to make sure the person actually registered.

The computer could at any time churn out the names of these unregistered people who wanted to support Republican candidates. The list could be sent to the campaigns of the president and senator who were running that year. The candidates' staffers were told: "These people want to vote for you, but they aren't registered. You go out and register them."

Republican Outreach

Nor did the effort end with registration.

The computers allowed targeting for purposes other than registering likely Republican voters. Using polling, phone bank, and census information, the party could produce clusters of voters who would most likely be interested in specific issues. For example, a candidate for the Senate might find from his polls that he was running poorly among women forty-five and older who were single heads of households. His polling told him that this group was concerned about crime. The party lists enabled the candidate to locate the names and addresses of, say, 25,000 women in this category. A letter from the candidate on what he proposed to do about crime could then be targeted only to this group. The Colorado GOP political director, Kay Riddle, justified the effort. "It sounds impersonal and high tech, but actually what it allows us to do is to be very personal, to touch people about what they care about, to talk to them about their concerns, and then to relay that information back to our candidates and legislators."

A similar computerized targeting effort allowed the Republicans to identify potential supporters among an ethnic group that tended to be strongly Democratic. The Republican National Committee developed a list of about 12,000 Hispanic last names. Those names were run against voter registration lists, then cross-tabbed against real estate tax lists. This allowed the party to identify unregistered Hispanics who were homeowners. That list could then be run against the names of buyers of expensive cars, subscribers to financial newspapers, and Hispanic businessmen. The goal was to search for upper-income Hispanics likely to identify with conservative Republican positions. Political director Riddle put it this way: "Our initial target has to be the upwardly mobile Hispanic who has a vision of the future that is similar to Ronald Reagan's. That takes a very sophisticated effort. . . ."

It also took money. The national GOP paid an estimated $7 for every new registered voter, for an estimated $10 million that year. The Democratic efforts, on the other hand, depended on non-party organizations registering the poor and minorities in grassroots drives. These were neither controlled nor usually paid for directly by the Democratic party. As a result, no one could be quite sure that the new Democratic registrants actually voted on Election Day.

The Republicans, for their part, had this problem covered by technology and more traditional techniques as well. The GOP designed follow-through programs that included get-out-the-vote (GOTV) drives, absentee ballots, and partisan direct mail. No one would be accusing the party of sitting on their bottoms on the critical day. A state GOP official commented: "We are not going to pay $5 for every new Republican and then let that person stay at home on Election Day. We are going to check those names against our computers all day on November 6, and if some guy hasn't shown up by 6 p.m., we'll carry him to the polls."

Blogs, Governor Dean, and the 2004 Election

Fast-forward twenty years to a different state, the other party, and a new technology. Former governor Howard Dean of Vermont is the come-from-nowhere candidate for the 2004 Democratic presidential nomination. But in January 2003 the governor is sounding a bit desperate. Talking with Joe Trippi, his campaign manager, Dean is upset that despite the crowds that are flocking to their events they have only $157,000 in the bank.

"We will never have any money," the governor complains.

"We have to use the Internet to build the base," Trippi responds.

While Governor Dean understands the concept, the details escape him. "What's a blog?" he asks.

Trippi knows the answer because, having burned out on politics, he had left Washington to spend time in California as a marketing consultant for dot-coms. While there he became a fan of "blogs"—short for Web logs—sites where thousands of people— bloggers—can post thoughts and commentaries. These Web soapboxes allow rapid responses in a never-ending virtual town-hall meeting. Trippi wondered whether such Internet communities could be used for an Internet-based presidential campaign. He also wondered whether this might help solve some of his party's disadvantages in competing for the presidency.[4]

The Democratic party entered the 2004 presidential season behind the Republicans in both organization and technology. Nowhere was this gap more apparent than in fundraising. In the recent 2000 election cycle, Republican party committees raised $692 million while Democrats raised $513 million. The GOP lead was even greater in money from small donors that in regulated limits could go directly to candidates. In this category of so-called "hard money," the

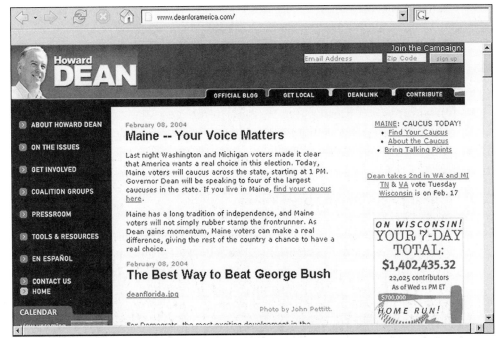

Howard Dean's website proved enormously helpful to his campaign, just not sufficient for victory.
The Image Works Archive/Courtesy the Democratic National Committee

Republicans raised $447 million to $270 million for Democrats.[5] And this was in a presidential year when the Democrats controlled the White House, which ought to make fundraising that much easier. Both in that year and again in 2004, Republican George W. Bush was so confident of his fundraising strength that he withdrew from federal matching funds in his primary campaigns so he wouldn't have to conform to spending limits and regulations. Democrats faced 2004 with a hard-earned sense of their vulnerability in fundraising.

And yet the Democratic party and its candidates did extraordinarily well raising money in the 2004 election cycle—mostly due to the antagonism toward President Bush, but also in part because of the Democrats' creative use of the Internet. It's virtually impossible to talk about the Internet in the 2004 presidential election without talking about Howard Dean. Although he lost the Democratic nomination, Dean's use of the Web to raise money and recruit volunteers may prove a model for future presidential efforts.

Prior to the 2004 elections the most frequent use of the Internet was easy to overlook—research. There was no faster or more economical way for a campaign to gather information than to go online. And numerous websites had sprung up to meet these needs, from *Opensecrets.org* (for information on money in politics) to *FirstGov.gov* (for federal government data).

Internet fundraising had increased with each election. An estimated 2 percent of donations came from online appeals in 1998, while some 10 percent was raised over the Internet in 2000. The most notable example in the 2000 presidential campaign was Republican John McCain raising $6 million after his surprise win over George W. Bush in the New Hampshire primary. The ability to raise a large amount of money in a short period of time made the Internet an accepted new weapon in campaign arsenals.

Climbing Aboard the e-Team

Howard Dean's campaign improved on the existing Internet fundraising and organizing techniques. Beginning as an unknown without a national fundraising network, Dean was able to raise $41 million in 2003, breaking President Bill Clinton's party record for money raised in one quarter of a year. His opposition to the war in Iraq gave him a clear, anti-establishment message that attracted intense supporters to his campaign. His exciting high-tech call to arms mobilized small donors to contribute via e-mail.[6]

The Dean campaign enlisted the help of two Internet companies. The first, Meetup.com, set up gatherings for people with common interests. The company focused on nonpolitical groups (breast-cancer survivors, for example), sorting names by zip code and setting up local "meetups" for them. The second, a nonprofit liberal Web group, MoveOn.org, also signed on. Originally created to organize people against Clinton's impeachment ("Censure President Clinton and move on"), MoveOn.org had a large e-mail list that they had successfully used for fundraising for liberal causes. They offered their expertise to all the Democratic candidates. Only the Dean campaign responded.

These two companies helped the campaign put together user-friendly blogs as electronic hangouts to mobilize like-minded Dean supporters. People could communicate directly with the campaign and with each other. In addition, these sites offered a range of online organizing tools—a directory of supporters, a site that enabled them to find and schedule their own events, and a link to Meetup.com. This last helped Dean people in scattered places find one another. They used online relationships, existing friendships, and two-way conversations to recruit supporters. Most of this was done from the ground up, with little or no direction from the top campaign leaders. Bloggers recruited other "Deaniacs," as Dean's committed supporters were dubbed. As campaign manager Trippi put it, "The Howard Dean movement, whatever it was, had taken on a life of its own, becoming a living, breathing organism . . . like concentric circles on steroids."[7]

The campaign's blogs created and mobilized a community among 165,000 dispersed supporters. They brought a national campaign to an effective local level by allowing like-minded partisans to do things like:

- type in a zip code and you meet Dean-inclined neighbors (photos often included).
- write a thirty-second anti-Bush television commercial, vote on which one of dozens you like, and then help raise $5 million in six weeks to air the winning advertisement.
- use search tools to locate one of three Mormon-centered pages to find an answer to the question "Can Mormons be Democrats?"
- leave your computer screen to hunt down unwired supporters and gather together at face-to-face meetings, somewhat like the "flash mob" craze where people using the Internet converge at the same public place as a prank.[8]

Internet organizing also raised a lot of money. In a few days in June 2003, the campaign got tens of thousands of donors to give nearly $3 million, doubling the campaign's take for that quarter. The Internet gave donors the ability to respond immediately to a TV or radio interview, or to unscripted "reality" video clips of the candidate shown on a website, *HowardDean.tv*. The donations kept increasing, with nearly half of the money raised coming from contributions of less than $200. Internet fundraising was also cost-efficient, netting more than 95 cents for every dollar given.[9]

The Internet's Future

Howard Dean ended up losing his race for the Democratic nomination, and rather badly. He lost early primaries and caucuses in Iowa and New Hampshire, and soon dropped out. But before that happened, an unknown governor of a small state had led in opinion polls and raised more money than any other Democrat. The failure of Dean's campaign led some to question the value of the Internet strategy. Arguably, his reliance on the Internet reinforced his image as a fringe anti-war candidate. But his collapse can also be linked to a brash personality and lack of local organizing in key primary and caucus states. Had Dean's use of the Internet changed presidential politics?

Dean's blogs shifted the fundraising emphasis from interest groups to individual donors. His fundraising opened the possibility that the Democrats, who have traditionally depended on wealthy contributors—mostly unions, trial lawyers, and some ethnic groups—could reorient their party toward small donors at the local grassroots. To some this meant that the party of the Left could return to the progressive politics of the past, uncoupled from its dependence on Washington interest groups, perhaps even bringing alienated young people back to the party. Whatever the future held, the 2004 presidential campaigns produced the most expensive election in history, with both campaigns approaching a billion dollars each in money received. In the money raised by the party committees, the Republicans still out-raised the Democrats, but not by much—$890 million to $817 million.[10] Newspaper reports attributed some of the candidates' fundraising success to their use of the Internet, although it still represented a minority of the contributions. Underlining the importance Democrat John Kerry gave to his Web network was that he first revealed his choice of vice president in the summer of 2004 to his million online supporters.[11]

The Dean campaign showed the potential for channeling blog links into electoral politics. Committed people reaching out through the Internet to allies could mobilize a national movement. But successfully combining the energy and outrage of social networks with the broad coalitions needed to influence national politics undoubtedly requires organizing beyond the Internet. One warning heard is that this technology offers the narrowing experience of an echo chamber, accelerating the polarized politics evident in the 2004 election. As "back alley media," Web ads and online news expressed views that might be considered out of place in mainstream media. Of course, the more partisan the Web chatter, the easier it was to persuade party members to write a check.

The citizen participation that this technology encourages may still be a step forward. If TV can be blamed for reducing political participation and encouraging a passive audience of stay-at-home viewers of advertisements and sound bites, then this new technology may do the reverse. As Joe Trippi optimistically concludes, "The Internet puts back into the campaign what TV took out—people."[12]

In Conclusion—The Partisan Politics of Technology

The Republican party took the lead in adapting technology to campaigns. As one book on technology and political parties concluded, "The Republicans pioneered most of the current applications, and the Democrats followed their lead."[13] This continued a global tradition of conservative parties using technology to compete with liberal opponents. Historically, party organizations were developed on the Left as a means of mobilizing the power of numbers in the working class against the material resources of conservative parties on the Right. The response on the Right to the Left's advantage in numbers (there are always more poor than rich people) was to build disciplined party organizations, using the most modern methods that money could buy. This expensive technology became an important advantage in the competition between wealthy interests and their more numerous opponents.[14] Colorado Republicans understood the point.

Technology works. The Republican abilities in targeting voters and turning them out on Election Day enhanced their chances against the majority Democrats. The mark of success for these techniques occurred ten years after the GOP's Colorado campaign. In a dramatic, and unexpected, shift in the power of the two parties, and one not unrelated to their advantage in using election technology, the Republicans in 1994 won elections that propelled them to a majority in both houses of Congress.

Arriving late to the party, the Democrats admitted that they were "blindsided by technology" and had to "catch up." And they did, first by using voter targeting and computer technology in much the same way as the Republicans did, and more recently in exploring the potential of the Internet. In Howard Dean, the party found a way to go beyond TV ads to reach individual citizens, encouraging them to participate and give money. The current Democratic embrace of the Internet (and of Howard Dean himself as the new chairman of the Democratic National Committee) shows that the creative use of technology is not a monopoly of either party.

Notes

1. David Broder, *The Party's Over: The Failure of American Parties* (New York: Harper and Row, 1971).
2. See Paul S. Herrnson, "Field Work, Political Parties, and Volunteerism," in James A. Thurber and Candice J. Nelson, eds., *Campaigns and Elections: American Style* (Boulder, CO: Westview Press, 1995), Chapter 12.
3. The Colorado case is based on Thomas B. Edsall and Haynes Johnson, "Colorado's High-Tech Republicans," in Roger H. Davidson and Walter J. Oleszek, eds., *Governing* (Washington, DC: Congressional Quarterly Press, 1987), 108–113.
4. Jeanne Cummings, "Behind the Dean Surge: A Gang of Bloggers and Webmasters," *Wall Street Journal*, October 14, 2003.
5. *Washington Post*, March 5, 2001.
6. See Joe Trippi, *The Revolution Will Not Be Televised* (New York: ReganBooks, 2004).
7. Trippi, 94. See also *The Hill*, November 26, 2003; Thomas B. Edsall, "Dean Sparks Debate on His Potential to Re-mold Party," *Washington Post*, October 20, 2003; Samantha M. Shapiro, "The Dean Connection," *New York Times Magazine*, December 7, 2003.
8. Frank Rich, "Napster Runs for President in '04," *New York Times*, December 21, 2003; Todd S. Purdom, "So What Was *That* All About?" *New York Times*, January 24, 2004; Brian Falter, "Dean Leaves Legacy of Online Campaign," *Washington Post*, February 20, 2004.

9. See Trippi.

10. See *www.opensecrets.org?presidential/index.asp.*

11. *New York Times,* July 2, 2004, A14.

12. As quoted by Frank Rich, "Napster Runs for President in '04," *New York Times,* December 21, 2003.

13 Stephen E. Frantzich, *Political Parties in the Technological Age* (New York: Longman, 1989), 222.

14. See Benjamin Ginsberg, "Money and Power: The New Political Economy of American Elections," in Thomas Ferguson and Joel Rogers, eds., *The Political Economy* (Armonk, NY: M. E. Sharpe Publishers, 1984).

chapter 8

Harry & Louise vs. Bill & Hillary

An Interest Group Goes Public

"Going public" is a strategy that aims to visibly demonstrate national support for an issue by mobilizing popular opinion. This strategy is used by presidents, by political parties, and by interest groups. One common way of going public is through the media, both by advertising and by influencing news coverage. Another tactic involves grassroots lobbying, which includes contacting supporters in states of key officials and getting them to communicate, by phone, mail, Internet, or visits, with their representatives. Both sets of tactics require a forceful message that expresses your side's strength and the other side's weakness.

In the following case of health care reform, both sides "go public." In 1993, President Bill Clinton, propelled by his recent election and bolstered by positive public opinion polls, eagerly embraces a national campaign to endorse his number one legislative priority, health care reform. Confronting him are health industry groups, fearful of their own future under the massive reform proposals, who use their ample resources to target national audiences to oppose the president's proposals. In also "going public," they joined with partisan rivals of the president to push a popular message that whipped up fears that expanding government bureaucracies would ruin the existing health care system.

The outcome was by no means guaranteed.

concepts highlighted

1. The **expansion of interest groups** is often related to the expansion of the fed-eral government. This case shows the organized responses of industry groups threatened by a major government reform of health care. Note the groups that took the lead in organizing against the reform. Was this a cross section of the entire health care industry? Who represents the consumers/public, or is that what the debate is about?

2. **Going public** is a strategy to overcome policy roadblocks in Washington. In this case, neither side was certain of the results of a battle in Congress, and both sides saw the need to mobilize national forces behind their position. How did interest groups ensure that their *media advertising* and *grassroots organizing* would have an impact on their Washington targets? Compare the advantages of both sides as they entered the battle.

3. One major battle between the sides was over **framing the issue**: Who would present the stakes of reform to the public in a convincing way? What were the competing frames used by the reformers and the health industry? What sort of media and grassroots communications did the interest groups oppos-ing reform use in presenting their arguments? How did their conservative allies influence the arguments that were used by the interest groups?

4. **Media coverage** clearly had an impact on how the public viewed and under-stood reform. How did the media coverage change over time? Did the media fail in its coverage by presenting the issue as a horserace and by being dis-tracted by charges of presidential scandals? How successful were the two sides in influencing the media?

5. What was the **influence of public opinion** on the outcome? Was the goal of going public designed to change public opinion or to mobilize support among those already convinced? Why did a popular president fail to win over public opinion?

The TV ad opens on a middle-aged couple, Harry and Louise, sitting around a kitchen table. They look puzzled. He is reading a newspaper, and she is examining a copy of President Clinton's health care plan. Harry pipes up:

"I'm glad the president's doing something about health care reform." *Louise replies,* "He's right. We need it."

But as the two learn new details about the president's plan, the conversation turns more critical.

Harry: *"Some of these details."*

Louise: *"Like a national limit on health care?"*

Harry: *"Really."*

Louise: *"The government caps how much the country can spend on all health care and says, 'That's it!'"*

Harry: *"So, what if our health plan runs out of money?"*

Louise: *"There's got to be a better way."*

Two actors playing Harry and Louise get their message out against health care reform in this TV ad.
Courtesy of the Health Insurance Association of America, Washington, DC

Paid for by the Health Insurance Association of America (HIAA), this simple ad, filmed in a kitchen and known in political circles as "Harry and Louise," first ran in early September 1993—even before President Clinton announced his plan for health care reform.

Later that month President Bill Clinton stood before Congress and a national television audience to launch the most important program of his young presidency. He promised universal health care—". . . giving every American health security—health care that's always there, health care that can never be taken away." In stirring words, the president made the need clear. "Our health care system takes 35 percent more of our income than any other country, insures fewer people, requires more Americans to pay more and more for less and less, and gives them fewer choices. There is no excuse for that kind of system, and it's time to fix it."

The issue was joined, the battle lines set. The "Harry and Louise" ad challenged the American president's views of health care reform before a national audience. In the president's view, reform was a courageous effort to mend a broken, inadequate health care system that left millions uncovered. In the eyes of industry groups, a power-hungry, inept federal bureaucracy was threatening to ruin a health care system that was the envy of the world. Which message the public accepted would go far to determine the outcome of reform in Washington.

These arguments reflected a paradox that existed in the public. By September 1993, a large majority of Americans wanted the federal government to solve the nation's perceived health care crisis. At the same time, equally large majorities had little faith in the federal government's capacity to act effectively. These contradictory views were behind the central messages delivered by the two sides of the national debate.

Inevitably, an expansion in government as large as Clinton proposed set off a defensive reaction from within the billion-dollar health care industry. Numerous interest groups began to lobby, organize, and advertise against the reforms. In this sense, the reformers motivated their opposition—the anti–health reform forces. In the end, the ironic result of the administration's far-reaching proposals was to strengthen their opponents.

Both sides pursued a strategy of going public by mobilizing national opinion to support their positions. The new president, fresh from a successful national election campaign, was comfortable in communicating with a broad public. Clinton expected that being in the White House would only increase his public support. Opponents of reform had less choice. The Democrats' control of both elected branches made Washington appear to be hostile territory. The health care interest groups were aided by their money, their experience with the issues, and their alliance with conservatives who saw partisan advantage in helping them. Underlying these advantages was the intensity of an industry with its back to the wall and its vital interests threatened.[1]

Health Security: Alive on Arrival

In his campaign for president, Bill Clinton had pledged to make health care reform a central goal of his first 100 days in office. It was a popular position. The United States had long trailed other industrialized countries in providing universal medical coverage. Because most health coverage was dependent on having a full-time job with benefits, those who were unemployed, in part-time jobs, or poor often had no insurance coverage. This included 15 percent of all Americans. For Clinton, Health Security was as important for the poor as Social Security was for senior citizens. Indeed, in a simplifying sound bite, the president held up a Health Security card that would function just like everyone's Social Security card.

In his speech of September 22, Clinton laid out one of the most comprehensive domestic policy proposals ever made by a president. The 1,364-page plan included a guarantee of universal health care coverage, a requirement that employers pay about 80 percent of the insurance costs, the creation of a national health board that would establish national spending limits, and insurance reforms prohibiting cutting benefits to people with preexisting medical conditions. Clinton's plan was a middle-of-the-road approach—a compromise between market-oriented and government-centered reforms.

Initial popular and press response was enthusiastic. A *Washington Post*/ABC nationwide poll after the speech found 67 percent approved of the president's program, while only 20 percent disapproved. An opposition Republican senator predicted, "We will pass a law next year." A *New York Times* headline read, "The Clinton Plan Is Alive on Arrival."[2]

But there were clouds on the horizon. The reform had been drawn up in secret by a huge White House task force headed by First Lady Hillary Clinton and Ira Magaziner, a bright, politically inexperienced friend of the president. The working group devising the complicated plan was isolated from many of the policy groups in and around government that were needed to pass the plan in Congress. These interests and experts, who should have been strong allies, felt alienated from the process. Though the First Lady was an effective advocate for reform, her presence inhibited internal debate: Who wanted to go to the president to complain about his wife?

Meanwhile, the opponents of reform were not sitting still. With the trillion-dollar health care industry representing one-fifth of the nation's economy, there were a number of wealthy interest groups with stakes in the outcome of the struggle. Small businesses, health insurers, drug companies, hospital associations, doctors, and chambers of commerce all mobilized money, ads, and lobbyists for the fight.

Republicans were strongly opposed for reasons beyond health care. Many from the moderate wing of the party favored passing some reform. But they were overwhelmed by the conservatives in their party, who viewed the Clinton program as a perfect target for their case against the threats posed by Big Government—fewer freedoms, more taxes. (Dennis Hastert, who would become Speaker of the House in 1999, described the plan in an oft-repeated sound bite as offering "the efficiency of the post office and the compassion of the IRS.") The campaign that followed energized conservative opinion nationwide. A year later the political momentum gained from defeating Clinton's proposal would aid the Republicans' triumphant takeover of Congress in the 1994 elections.

Opponents of Reform Go Public

As seen in the Harry and Louise ads, opponents of reform were not about to allow the White House to frame the terms of the debate. In the beginning, many businesses connected with health care wanted to negotiate the best deal they could for their industry. This stance reflected resignation to some reform passing. As the tide shifted against the Clintons, opponents jumped at the chance to defeat reform entirely. The battle polarized positions on both sides. Hillary Clinton attacked the health insurance industry (whose trade association funded Harry and Louise ads) for "price-gouging, cost-shifting and unconscionable profiteering."[3]

The health insurance industry led the private groups organizing against Clinton. The cutting edge of this effort was the Health Insurance Association of America (HIAA), a group of mid-sized and small insurance companies. These companies feared being forced out of business if the reforms passed. Although there were splits within the industry—with the more reform-minded large insurers, who thought they could survive reform, leaving HIAA—the insurers that remained in HIAA put their political savvy and money into an aggressive campaign of ads and grassroots organizing. Led by a respected former eight-term Republican congressman from Ohio, Willis D. Gradison, HIAA first tried for concessions and then attacked.

On the ad front, HIAA ran three installments of "Harry and Louise," emphasizing evolving themes and trying to wring changes in the health care plan from the administration. The association spent almost $15 million on these ads, a large share of the $50 million both sides spent on ads in the health care debate.[4] As one ad followed another, the white, middle-class couple uncovered the horrors of care-by-bureaucracy: It might run out of money; government would be choosing their health plan for them; and younger people could pay higher premiums. These ads framed the industry's arguments and amplified public uneasiness with a reform not being clearly explained by the White House.

Among followers of the black arts of political commercials, the Harry and Louise ads gained status because of their impressive impact. Actually, the ads were shown in only a few markets, mainly in the Washington–New York corridor. Their influence grew after Hillary Clinton attacked them. In a blistering November 1993 speech, she accused the insurance industry of lying to the public in order to protect profits. "They have the gall to run TV ads that there is a better way, the very industry that has brought us to the brink of bankruptcy because of the way they have financed health care," declared an unlady-like First Lady.

Inadvertently, Hillary's unplanned outburst increased the news coverage given the industry, a point underlined by HIAA's leader, Gradison: "What they did was to give our advertising a much larger audience than it would have had. . . ." The Clintons tried to make a joke out of "Harry and Louise" in a satiric skit at an annual dinner for Washington reporters at The Gridiron Club. President Clinton, representing the "Coalition to Scare Your Pants Off," played Harry. He asks, "You mean after Bill and Hillary put all those new bureaucrats and taxes on us, we're still all going to die?"[5] The result was still more attention for the ads.

Less visible than TV commercials, but arguably more effective, was the interest groups' grassroots organizing. Although dismissed as "AstroTurf" (or artificial grassroots), paid organizers mobilized public opinion in states and districts of key members of Congress. They recruited local business leaders, patients in doctors' offices, employees of drug companies, and hospital workers. These industry "stakeholders" were encouraged to write letters or phone or visit their elected representatives. Coalitions sprang up using networks of small businesspeople, insurance agents, and medical suppliers. Over $100 million was spent to hammer reform into the ground. In the words of the nonpartisan Center for Public Integrity, health care reform became in 1993 and 1994 "the most heavily lobbied legislative initiative in recent U.S. history."[6]

HIAA added commercials to their grassroots tactics. Advertising, both print and TV, focused on key battleground states, mostly those represented by conservative Democrats who would be sympathetic to the message. Every ad included a toll-free 800 number that people could call. Those calling would be entered into a database and urged to write letters or patched through to their member of Congress. (Patching allowed the interest group's phone bank to directly connect callers to their congressional office.) HIAA corralled 45,000 people, generating over a quarter of a million contacts with the media and Congress.[7]

The groups mobilizing to fight the Clinton plan were those with a direct economic stake and those with a more general conservative agenda. Besides the insurers, the Pharmaceutical Research and Manufacturers of America (PRMA) represented leading drug companies worried about price controls on drugs. They, along with the American Medical Association, sponsored numerous free trips for members of Congress. Business associations got involved, including those for large corporations—the Business Roundtable, and small businesses—the National Federation of Independent Business (NFIB). Lobbyists for grocery stores and chains like Burger King that hired many part-time workers without health insurance met frequently with legislators. Conservative groups such as the Christian Coalition sponsored newspaper ads. One featured a picture of a friendly family doctor giving a child shots for immunization, with the warning "Don't let a government bureaucrat in this picture."

This coalition of the health industry, business groups, deficit hawks, and social conservatives operated with a great deal of unity. They shared polls, exchanged intelligence, and targeted legislators needing special attention. They were supported by Republican party donor lists. They got their arguments on the *Wall Street Journal* editorial page. They listened to conservative talk radio's Rush Limbaugh for comic reassurance. And they took comfort from the spiritual backing of conservative churches. The ranks of these foes of reform hardened as the fight progressed.

The White House Campaign Stumbles

The White House effort to promote health care reform resembled a presidential campaign. Clinton, used the same consultants who had led the drive to the presidency. This excluded the health care experts within the government who lacked campaign experience. The tactics of an election also personalized the battle—focusing attention on the president and first lady—making it more partisan and expanding the fight into a nationwide media contest. What might have been a narrower Washington debate over legislation leading to a negotiated compromise instead became a bitter public wrestling match with clear winners and losers.[8]

One of the first problems the Clinton administration encountered was how to explain a very complex plan very simply. It was not the White House's fault that health care was, in fact, complicated—Reform was hard enough to explain to legislators with experience in the health care field. It was even more difficult to explain to a skeptical media and a public that wanted reform but feared government "bungling."

White House hopes to use the president to dominate the national news with health care would soon be derailed. Following his speech, the president planned to devote a month to promoting the program, with rallies across the country, leading up to submitting it to Congress in October. But overseas crises intervened. A failed raid in Somalia resulted in eighteen dead American soldiers and brutal televised pictures of a GI's body dragged through the streets. A noisy demonstration in Haiti embarrassingly stopped an American warship from docking. Overheated news from Russia reported the new post-Communist regime of Boris Yeltsin teetering on the brink. These crises demanded the president's attention. In October he had to cancel all but one of his health care events. A month that was to launch the campaign instead weakened the president's connection with health care along with its prospects.

Scandals, real and manufactured, plagued the Clintons. The death in July 1993 of Vincent Foster, a White House aide and close friend of the First Family, sparked widespread conspiracy theories. Although investigated and ruled a suicide, Vince Foster's "murder" became a staple of right-wing radio talk shows. Even more distractions came from the investigations by congressional committees and special prosecutors into the Clintons' Arkansas land dealings, known as Whitewater. Although the Clintons were never ultimately charged with anything illegal, the turmoil took its toll. It diverted the White House by dominating the headlines ("Whitewater: More Questions Than Answers," "How Bad Is It?" etc.). And it weakened the president's ability to communicate on issues—like health care. The president's opponents took advantage of the charges. Conservative talk-show host Rush Limbaugh told his audience of mil-

Hillary and Bill get the message out for health care reform from the White House.
© Wally McNamee/Corbis

lions, "I think Whitewater is about health care. . . . If people are going to base their support for the plan on whether they can take his [the president's] word, I think it's fair to examine whether or not he keeps his word."[9]

The Battle Joined, and Broadcast

Because of the political storms swirling around the White House, the pro-reform forces found themselves fragmented and outspent, with difficulty unifying their coalition. Part of the problem was stated afterward by the president: ". . . The supporters were always thinking about how they could get a better deal." For example, the powerful AARP (American Association of Retired Persons) was later criticized for questioning the details of the plan instead of immediately campaigning in support. By spring of 1994, when they finally spent $5 million to back reform, it was too late.

During the crucial months following the president's speech—October to December 1993—the opposition had the advertising field to themselves. Groups like the Democratic National Committee were decisively outspent. In this period, the DNC spent just $150,000 for ads, while HIAA and PRMA anteed up $17.5 million for TV and print ads. With the president being distracted by crises and opponents spending a ton of money, it was the enemies of health care that got to define the message early to the public.

The media helped. Intentionally or not, the press coverage emphasized the political fight over health care, rather than the substance of the reform and how it would personally affect American families. The emphasis on conflict was considered more exciting, as well as easier to cover. Already noted was how much the media commented on and repeated opposition ads like Harry and Louise. Much of the coverage emphasized the impact of these ads on public opinion, "creating real doubts" among the general public about the Clinton program. Of course, *reporting* widespread doubts about reform looked to supporters the same as *spreading* widespread doubts.

Part of the problem the press faced was the sheer complexity of the plan. One correspondent for the *Los Angeles Times* said she felt "swamped by the immensity of the policy stuff and the political dimensions. It was so complicated. . . ." When asked how well the administration had explained the plan she added, "They were awful. The plan was virtually unexplainable, and at first they were just arrogant. . . . Pretty soon, it was all being lost in confusion and fear."[10]

A study of press coverage appearing in the *Columbia Journalism Review* found that the public had actually become *less* informed on the basics of the proposal as the campaign progressed.[11] This development followed the shift in media focus from the seriousness of the health care crisis to the conflicts surrounding reform. Exceptional efforts by the press to explain the reforms—such as NBC-TV's June 1994 two-hour, prime-time, commercial-free program on health care, financed by a foundation grant—didn't have much impact. As less attention was paid to the consequences of this reform for families, the public ended up getting most of its information from special-interest sources. Much of it was slanted. James Fallows, a respected journalist, called the health care battle "the press's Vietnam War," arguing that "the media failed in a historic way to help Americans understand and decide on this issue."[12]

Post-Operative Postscripts

By mid-1994 it was over. There were vain attempts among moderate Democrats and Republicans to compromise, by passing parts of the president's reform. But despite Democratic control of Congress, despite the commitment from the Oval Office, and despite months of effort by supporters in unions, health care institutions, and non-profits, Washington couldn't move on universal health coverage.

On September 26, 1994, almost exactly a year after Clinton had addressed Congress, Senate Democratic Leader George Mitchell made the announcement: A compromise on health care reform would not be brought up. The Senate majority leader said, "The combination of the insurance industry on the outside and a majority of Republicans on the inside proved to be too much to overcome." The reform never even reached the floor of Congress for a vote. It was a stunning defeat.

One skeptic defined historians as prophets looking backward. It is a warning of how easy it is to look at past political fights like that over health care reform and make the losers look incompetent, the winners invulnerable, and the outcome inevitable. But to the participants, very little is preordained. President Clinton's assessment of his defeat is one place to start. "Any time you try to change something that's big and complicated, the people who are against it have a better argument because they can be simple and straight. That's number one. Number two, any time you've got something that touches people where they live—and health care is profoundly important to everybody—it's easier for people to be frightened than it is for people to live on their hopes."

The president was insightful without being complete. The opposition's bleak message of fearing Big Government did contribute to the outcome. But the political activities of the messengers were also central. Richard Gephardt, Democratic House majority leader and a commander of the Clinton forces, gave the opponents a backhanded compliment when he downplayed the impact of money on his side's defeat. "It's not money. It's votes. . . . I think money had little to do with the outcome. It's the political work they do at home."[13]

Note that Gephardt was referring to the votes of politicians and the grassroots work done in their districts and states. These committed interest groups convinced elected officials that health reform was not politically viable. They used the modern techniques of public politics to change the views of elected officials in Washington. In his book *Going Public,* Samuel Kernell wrote, "Intense minorities scare politicians more than inattentive majorities for the good reason that the former will act on their beliefs and the latter will not."[14] In this sense President Clinton was wrong. It was not the public that was scared by the campaign against health care reform. It was the politicians.

That conclusion is reinforced by the fact that the campaigns may not have changed public opinion on the core issues. From beginning to end, over 70 percent of those polled agreed with the two fundamental goals behind the Clinton reform. One was that all American families should have health insurance. The other was that employers should contribute to paying for their workers' premiums. Thus, even with their uncertainty about the government's ability to deliver on reform, a majority of Americans favored the changes in health care that Clinton was proposing. This striking majority remained unaltered by the campaigns.[15]

What did change was *political* opinion toward Clinton's plan. Control over the national agenda on health care was wrestled away from the new president by a coalition of conservatives and health industry groups. They spread the dubious messages that reform would mean more bureaucracy, less freedom to choose a doctor, and lower-quality care at higher cost. The coalition's commercials, grassroots activities, and lobbying had a critical part. The White House and its supporters failed to respond with a clear, compelling story in favor of reform. President Clinton was hampered by foreign crises, over-hyped scandals, and a process too tightly controlled by his wife and close allies. The media failed to explain the substance of the program and focused on political infighting.

Harry and Louise played their role as well. By the summer of 1994, the reformers' loss of control over public opinion was underlined, ironically, by a Democratic commercial. In July, toward the end of the policy debate, the Democratic National Committee began airing a new TV ad called "Harry Takes a Fall." In the spot, Harry and Louise are in bed. Harry is in a full body cast while Louise's arm is in a sling. Harry has lost his job, his health insurance, and most of his wealth. Louise is blaming Harry for opposing reform. While they helped the Democrats make their argument, Harry and Louise were sending another message: They were now defining the issue for their opponents. Even in politics, imitation is the sincerest form of flattery.[16]

Notes

1. For the perspective of the president in going public, see Samuel Kernell, *Going Public: New Strategies of Presidential Leadership,* 3rd ed. (Washington, DC: Congressional Quarterly Press, 1997). For the view of the interest groups, see Allan J. Cigler and Burdett A. Loomis, eds., *Interest Group Politics,* 5th ed. (Washington, DC: Congressional Quarterly Press, 1999).

2. Darrell M. West and Burdett Loomis, *The Sound of Money: How Political Interests Get What They Want* (New York: W. W. Norton, 1999).

3. Haynes Johnson and David S. Broder, *The System* (Boston: Little, Brown and Company, 1997), 202.

4. West and Loomis.

5. Johnson and Broder, 211.

6. As quoted by Theda Skocpol, *Boomerang: Health Care Reform and the Turn Against Government* (New York: W. W. Norton, 1997), 141.

7. West and Loomis, 85.

8. See Johnson and Broder, Chapter 24, "Lessons: Lost Opportunities."

9. Johnson and Broder, 276.

10. Johnson and Broder, 230.

11. Johnson and Broder, 230.

12. See James Fallows, *Breaking the News* (New York: Vintage Books, 1997), "The Press's Vietnam War," 205–234.

13. Johnson and Broder, 198.

14. Kernell, 213.

15. Johnson and Broder, 631. More detailed and more negative conclusions about public opinion on health care reform can be found in Lawrence R. Jacobs and Robert Y. Shapiro, *Politicians Don't Pander* (Chicago: University of Chicago Press, 2000), Chapter 7.

16. West and Loomis, 105–106.

chapter 9

Media and the Lewinsky Scandal

A Perfect Storm

genda-setting and *framing* are two major ways that the media influence politics. Of the many challenges facing the country, those in the headlines or on TV are usually seen by the public and officials as deserving to be on the nation's agenda. If the press discusses crime often and hunger only slightly, for example, crime will likely be seen as a higher priority. This is known as agenda-setting. Framing defines problems. It shapes *how* the public sees an issue. The framing of an event or a person presents one of many possible reading of the facts. "By choosing a common frame to describe an event, condition, or political personage, journalists shape public opinion."[1] Media coverage can frame a subject in many ways. Is crime linked to unemployment or to lax immigration laws, for example? How the press tells a story influences how the topic of the story is understood. In the following case, other political actors besides journalists try to frame coverage to serve their interests.

The concepts of agenda-setting and framing surface in this case. The media placed President Bill Clinton's affair with White House intern Monica Lewinsky on the nation's agenda and escalated it into a mega-scandal that led to Clinton's impeachment. The scandal dominated the nation's attention for a year. During that time, different frames arose for understanding the issues in the competition to shape public opinion. Supporters of the president attacked the partisan motives of his accusers and claimed the scandal had no impact on his official duties. Opponents linked the affair to lying under oath and the president's immorality. The media generally framed the scandal as a continuing pattern of adultery and dishonesty, deserving of sanction. The public rejected the media's interpretation, separating Clinton's private indiscretions from their robust approval of his job as president.

The Lewinsky scandal shows the power and limits of media. The press could headline the events and keep them in front of the public and its leaders. Aligned

Thanks to Edward Wasserman for his comments on an early draft of this chapter.

with partisan forces, they could drive the political process to the point of impeachment. Aggressive new media outlets on cable and the Internet expanded their audiences by saturating the airways with 24/7 coverage of the scandal. Yet in their "feeding frenzy" the media increasingly looked like racy tabloids— unreliable as news sources. The public, turned off by both the coverage and the use of it for political advantage, reached its own collective judgment that a sex scandal should not undermine a popular president.

concepts highlighted

1. In placing the scandal before the nation as an important issue, the media engaged in **agenda-setting**. To what degree was this a conscious decision of people in the media, or to what extent did the scandal "take on a life of its own" in a "feeding frenzy" of competitive journalism?
2. In **framing** the scandal, the media presented it as part of Clinton's pattern of dishonest behavior that interfered with his official duties. Note how the first press coverage made this link by connecting the affair to testifying under oath. Why didn't this frame seem to convince the public?
3. How was the coverage of the scandal affected by the **economics of the media**? Look for issues of competition between new and old media; promotion of inexpensive talk shows; and broadcast media depending on stories revealed first by print journalists.
4. **White House news management** attempted to protect the president. How did the White House "spin" the coverage in a more favorable light, use leaks to attack opponents, and present the president going about his official duties unaffected by the controversy? How important was the president's celebrity personality? How did political opponents of the president use the media? Why weren't they more successful?
5. This case illustrates **adversarial journalism**—the often conflicted relationship between politicians and reporters. Does news that can attract a wide audience give the media an interest in emphasizing political scandals? Is there any liberal or conservative bias in this case of the press's adversarial coverage?

The Lewinsky scandal engulfing the Clinton administration in 1998 was the "perfect" political storm: an unusual buildup of forces that came together to create a public hurricane. It began with the most common of elements—a talkative, love-struck young woman, an ambitious secretary, a relentless reporter, a flawed powerful man—swept up into a charged partisan atmosphere. Aggressive prosecutors saw the scandal as an opportunity to energize their stalled investigation of the president's real estate dealings. The press, fueled by leaks and competition from cable TV and the Internet, heated the atmosphere with twenty-four-hour coverage. The destructive, lurid disclosures and the fury from colliding forces held the public's attention for over a year. Yet ultimately the energy generated from the tempest had little lasting impact. The storm ended calmly in a Senate vote staged under the protective traditions of impeachment.

A Charged Atmosphere

Mike Isikoff's compact energy unbalanced a charged atmosphere. The *Newsweek* reporter could be fairly described as a bit obsessed with Bill Clinton's sex life. He had pursued this angle since he worked for the *Washington Post*. It had cost him his job. In 1994 he had battled for months to get his editors to publish Arkansas state employee Paula Jones's charges that Clinton had propositioned her in a Little Rock hotel room. Eventually the *Post* became the first major newspaper to print Jones's account of her encounter with the then-governor of Arkansas. But the shouting matches that the awkward, combative reporter had with his bosses led to his suspension, and eventually Isikoff left the paper. Now, in early 1998, he was having a similar battle with his editors at *Newsweek*.

For a year Isikoff had been investigating a story of the president's affair with a young White House intern named Monica Lewinsky. Through Isikoff's contacts from his reporting on Paula Jones, he had gotten to know Linda Tripp, a former White House secretary with ambitions to publish a gossipy book on the Clinton administration. Tripp had become friends with Monica Lewinsky when both were moved from the White House to jobs in the Pentagon. Lewinsky, as the public would soon learn, was the plump, pretty intern having an affair with the president. Not surprisingly, the twenty-four-year-old talked about it with friends. More surprisingly, one of these "friends" secretly taped their conversations. Convinced by her literary agent that she needed the "goods" to market her book (titled *The President's Women*) to a publisher, Linda Tripp had bought a $100 tape recorder, taped her friend, and gone to Isikoff with the results.[2]

The story up till now might well have taken its place with numerous other swirling scandals that Clinton had been sailing through for much of his political career. The most publicized charges had come from Gennifer Flowers, an Arkansas lounge singer. She had held a press conference, complete with recorded phone calls between the two, to announce that, yes, she had been Clinton's lover for more than a decade. For maximum impact, the press conference was staged during the 1992 primary race for the Democratic nomination. Surviving this required Clinton to appear on CBS News's *60 Minutes* holding hands with his wife, Hillary, to deny any intimate relationship—a half-truth at best, since Clinton admitted "having caused pain in his marriage"—but insisted he wanted to move on (what is known in the press as a "non-denial

denial"). Following that, other women surfaced with tears, tales, and tabloid contracts. There were enough of them for the public to believe Clinton practiced adultery, and for the press to disbelieve anything he said on the subject.

If the press was primed to distrust the president, others were out to prove him legally unfit for office. The office of the independent counsel with a mandate to investigate the president made this scandal different from the preceding ones. In mid-1994 Kenneth Starr had taken over as independent counsel investigating a shady land deal in Arkansas labeled Whitewater, in which the Clintons had invested. A previous special prosecutor had cleared the president, but the House and Senate banking committees insisted on reopening the investigation. Starr, who had held high-level positions in two Republican administrations, was backed by conservatives in hopes of a more aggressive inquiry into the Clinton administration. Friends of the president were indicted and later convicted. Although Clinton was never charged in Whitewater, his reputation was tarnished. Lurking in the background was a harassment suit brought against him in1994 by Paula Jones, with the financial and legal support of Clinton's political enemies. A federal judge ruled that because a president was immune from distracting civil cases, the lawsuit would have to wait until Clinton left office. But in January 1997 a unanimous Supreme Court held that a president wasn't immune; the suit against Clinton could go forward.

On January 17, Clinton testified before Paula Jones's lawyers, who had been briefed about his relationship with Lewinsky. Taken by surprise by their questions about Lewinsky, the president said he did not remember ever having been alone with her and denied having sexual relations with the intern. The day before the president's testimony, Starr had gotten permission from the attorney general to expand his investigation into charges that Clinton asked Lewinsky to lie under oath. Starr took the position that even if he was investigating one crime (Whitewater), if he discovered evidence of another (Lewinsky's perjury) he should investigate it. The president's testimony under oath would eventually lead to the charges of perjury and obstruction of justice that brought the scandal to impeachment. Shaped by Starr's aggressive legal team, the media's coverage of Clinton's lies and sexual indiscretions would grow into a fury.[3]

Media Feeding Frenzy

The New York Times *isn't leaving anything for us.*

An editor of the tabloid *National Enquirer*[4]

It was no coincidence that Paula Jones's lawyers had uncovered the Lewinsky affair. They had been getting anonymous calls suggesting that they subpoena Monica Lewinsky and Linda Tripp. The calls came from Tripp as a way to surface Lewinsky and put herself in the middle of the action.[5] When Lewinsky was subpoenaed to testify before Jones's lawyers in late 1997, she panicked. On the Tripp tapes, Lewinsky's hysteria reflected a fear that she would have to either betray the president or commit perjury. She chose the latter route and signed an affidavit on January 7 declaring that she never had an affair with the president. And Linda Tripp, her celebrity-driven motives consistent throughout this tale, went to Ken Starr on January 12. It was the Tripp tapes that allowed Starr to expand his investigation from Whitewater to Lewinsky, after first knowing that Paula Jones's lawyers had the information and would use it to trap the president.

Starr and his team of prosecutors treated Tripp as if they had *almost* won the lottery. They spent the night and the next day debriefing her. Starr needed to prove that the president had tried to get Lewinsky to lie about their affair, which was obstruction of justice—a felony. If Lewinsky was trapped into admitting her affair on tape, they would then pressure her to wear a wire, call the president, and get him on tape obstructing justice. In other words, Starr planned to put a "sting" on the president of the United States.

Having gotten the story from Tripp, Isikoff went to his editors at *Newsweek*, who were reluctant to publish it. Their problem was that on the Tripp tapes Monica never says, "Clinton told me to lie." In fact, at one point Tripp tries to get Monica to say that Clinton knows she's going to lie, and Monica says no. This divided the editors over whether to go ahead with publication. Starr offered *Newsweek* his cooperation—hence, a better story—if they waited.[6] By the next morning, the power of the new media to change press behavior was demonstrated. Matt Drudge, the gossipy writer of the "Drudge Report," had sent out a bulletin on his website that *Newsweek* had killed Isikoff's story about the president's affair with an intern. A media storm was growing out of anyone's control.

For the next few weeks, the stories poured out in a torrent from television, cable, radio, print, and the Internet. Much of this was built upon the Washington media's adversarial view of the Clinton administration as undisciplined and dishonest. At the very beginning of the young administration, one respected correspondent declared that covering the new White House was like "coming home and finding your kids got into the liquor cabinet."[7] But this attitude now became *a feeding frenzy* of attack journalism where the press goes after a wounded politician like sharks, "creating the news as much as reporting it. . . ."[8] In the words of journalist Bob Woodward, who exposed President Richard Nixon's sins in the 1970s, it was "a frenzy unlike anything you ever saw in Watergate. . . ."

By the Wednesday after the release of the "Drudge Report," the *Washington Post,* quoting "sources," led the mainstream press with an article revealing that Clinton directed Lewinsky to testify falsely. ABC's *Good Morning America*

There was little question what the news was in New York City on January 28, 1998.
AFP/AFP/Getty Images

reported that the president had instructed her to deny an affair. This coverage was an early example of questionable interpretations—citing proof of presidential wrongdoing from the same tapes that *Newsweek*'s editors listened to and didn't publish because they heard no such evidence. The "sources" were probably the president's opponents in the independent counsel's office. Starr's staff was publicly refusing to comment, claiming that they were not allowed to talk about a witness who might testify before a grand jury. Leaks were another matter.

The media deluge intensified. On ABC, George Stephanopoulos, the former Clinton aide, commented that if the allegations were true "it could lead to impeachment proceedings." CNN found a 10-second video clip showing the president hugging Lewinsky in a roped line of people at a White House lawn reception. It was aired hundreds of times, often in slow motion. MSNBC converted its coverage into what one critic called "all Monica, all the time."[9] Media economics played a role: Powered by the scandal, MSNBC used their talk-news programs to launch the new network into a profitable orbit. Their ratings increased 131 percent.

The "new media" (Internet, cable, and satellite) drove the frenzy, and without the restraint displayed by the mainstream media of TV networks, newspapers, and magazines. The opportunities to break a story on the Internet were unlimited, as demonstrated when the "Drudge Report" picked up Isikoff's rejected *Newsweek* story. The traditional media before this scandal would not break news on their websites, preferring to run stories that had first been reported in their major outlet. Now the mainstream press, starting with the *Washington Post*'s initial story, scooped the competition by putting the story online first. This development resulted in errors as well as an "echo effect." Repetition made outrageous claims credible.

Talk shows from *Larry King Live* to *Geraldo Rivera Live* mixed facts, fiction, speculation, and ax-grinding—with no one able to tell the difference. Political scientist John Anthony Maltese said, "Talk is easy and talk is cheap, and the proliferation of these shows led to saturation coverage of the Lewinsky story."[10] Rumors were everywhere. Conservative commentator Ann Coulter mentioned incidents with "four other interns." CNN's Wolf Blitzer reported from the White House lawn that Clinton's close aides were discussing his resignation. *NBC News* anchor Tom Brokaw broke into a pre–Super Bowl program with an "unconfirmed" report that Starr's office was investigating that someone saw the president and Lewinsky in an intimate moment. The *New York Post* declared that the Secret Service found the lovers, with a headline screaming, "Caught in the Act." The *Wall Street Journal* ran a story that a White House steward told a grand jury that he saw the two alone in a study and recovered tissues with physical evidence on them.

These reports were recycled in multiple public outlets in the first weeks as the media raced to keep the news flowing. And, though it may not have reduced their impact, all these stories were false.[11]

White House News Management: Shelter from the Storm

Whatever the flaws in the coverage, the fury of the media seemed unstoppable. At first, the White House seemed shell-shocked by the onslaught. As it collectively recovered its balance, aides tried to redirect the charges and protect the president.

On the Wednesday morning that the article in the *Washington Post* appeared, press secretary Mike McCurry, reading from notes, said Clinton was "outraged" by the reports and denied any improper relationship. When asked what he meant by an "improper relationship," McCurry refused to elaborate. As this was just the latest in Clinton's history of alleged marital affairs, most of the press assumed Clinton was lying. This became clear when he sat down for a scheduled interview with PBS's Jim Lehrer that afternoon and declared that "there is no sexual relationship." Reporters leaped: Why did the president use the present tense? Was he implying a past affair?[12]

Leaks poured out that undercut the White House denials. Clinton had sent Monica gifts, including a book of Walt Whitman poems; his voice was on her answering machine; and she mentioned visiting the White House on many evenings. The White House put its spin on the reports cascading down on them. When the subject couldn't be changed, the next best strategy was to attack: Blame the accusers, point to the right wing, refuse to release records, denounce the press. There were whispers that Lewinsky was emotionally unstable, that the tapes were doctored, and that Starr was out to "get" the president. Cabinet members defended the president's honesty, while aides denounced the "campaign of leaks and lies." Hillary attacked political opponents, which was an improvement over discussing her husband's sex life. Whipping up a public backlash against the press could only help the president. Attacking the special prosecutor for unauthorized leaks had the added benefit of truth to it.

One successful example of White House spin occurred when the *New York Times* reported that the president's secretary had told investigators for the independent counsel that Monica and the president had sometimes been alone and that the president had coached the secretary before she testified. The White House struck back. Avoiding the subject of the article, aides appeared on three network morning shows to denounce "these criminal leaks" from the prosecutor's office. (The *Times* reporters had discussed their report with Starr and his staff.) A Democratic congressman requested an investigation into illegally leaked grand jury evidence. That afternoon the president's lawyer gave a rare news conference. As the TV cameras rolled, he asked the federal courts to investigate leaks by Starr's office. The result was to shift the news of the scandal to the issue of leaks. That week *Time* and *Newsweek* put the leaks controversy on their covers.[13]

Internally there was a conflict between the political staff and the lawyers over how much the president should say in public. Ultimately they compromised. Clinton would make a forceful public denial but would not say anything new—which the lawyers preferred. On Monday morning, January 26, after an event publicizing child care needs, Clinton answered reporters' shouted questions. He jabbed his finger and emotionally declared, "I did not have sexual relations with *that woman,* Miss Lewinsky. I never told anybody to lie, not a single time." The following morning on the *Today* show, Hillary denounced

Starr as a "politically motivated prosecutor" and part of a "vast right-wing conspiracy," which the press in their "feeding frenzy" had joined. She refused to answer any questions about her husband's relationship with his intern.[14]

That night, January 27, President Clinton delivered the annual State of the Union address to Congress. With cheering Democrats in the audience and 53 million viewers at home, Clinton reminded Americans of their economic prosperity, of his proposals for the future, and of his stature as president. He never mentioned the scandal, implicitly making the point that such "private" behavior didn't belong in this national ritual of a chief of state. (As one White House aide later wrote: "Separating what Clinton was doing as president from the scandal became a basic strategy."[15]) A *Los Angeles Times* poll found that 75 percent of those asked rated the speech "good" or "excellent." Equally important, 67 percent said that it "kept my attention and I didn't think about the allegations against him." Sunlight seemed to have broken through the clouds over the White House.[16]

The Public Holds Its Nose and Applauds Its President—No Mean Trick

Public opinion was to prove the president's most powerful ally. Although some wavered at the beginning of the scandal, the public stuck with Bill Clinton, concluding that no, he had not told the truth, and yes, he should stay in office. Clinton's impressive public approval—among the highest of any modern president—steadily held in the mid-60 percent range and, at times, over 70 percent.[17]

Few would have predicted this support when the scandal first broke. Clinton rested at a respectable 60 percent in several polls at the time. By the end of the first week, his approval numbers had dropped to 51 percent. Sixty-two percent believed he had an affair with Lewinsky, and over half thought he had asked her to lie. Even worse for the president, 63 percent in a *Washington Post* poll thought he should resign if he had lied or had asked her to lie. If he had lied under oath and wouldn't resign, 55 percent supported impeachment.[18]

The media's framing the scandal as relevant to the president's official duties mattered less than people's assessment of the peace, prosperity, and moderation that Clinton's presidency represented. Media scholar Kathleen Hall Jamieson wrote that the public drew "a clear distinction between private and public character, between the personal and the presidential."[19] Most people viewed the scandal as the president's private behavior, not connected to his public life or their own lives. The line between public and private was bent (for instance, when the Starr Report released details of the Oval Office incidents), but held firm.

"They love him most for the enemies he has made" is a phrase taken from a nominating speech for another Democratic president, Grover Cleveland, in 1884. Clinton, too, benefited from his choice of enemies. It wasn't hard for the White House to frame the scandal as a political vendetta. The president's allies could point to Republicans' angry rhetoric and the GOP's inability to make congressional impeachment hearings bipartisan. By the fall, Republican leaders, including Speaker of the House, Newt Gingrich, were finding their own personal failings (adultery in Newt's case) being aired on Internet publications like *Salon*. Also helping Clinton was that the women in the scandal were hardly saints. Sympathy for Monica Lewinsky cooled as stories of a previous affair with a married man surfaced. Few believed Linda Tripp was motivated by patriotism and trying to help her "friend." Paula Jones seemed moved by monetary gain from right-wing benefactors. In spring 1998 while Clinton's favorable ratings were over 60 percent, House leader Gingrich stood at 36 percent, Starr at 22 percent, Monica 17 percent, and Tripp 10 percent. Ken Starr's approval ratings would drop later in the year to 11 percent, about the same as Saddam Hussein.[20]

By the time the surging scandal was channeled into the impeachment process, the Republicans were the big losers in public opinion. In October after the nearly party-line vote in the House to impeach, 62 percent of Americans polled disapproved of the Republican handling of the issue. During the Senate trial, disapproval of the process rose from 41 percent to 56 percent. Perhaps this was a result of an overly partisan media strategy by the GOP, or the popularity of the president, or the prosperity of the country. Or perhaps it was the result of simple disgust with the saturation coverage of a seedy event. The Washington bureau of the Associated Press moved 4,109 stories on the scandal in 1998 and had twenty-five reporters working regularly on it. In just that one year, there were 25,975 stories on the scandal in the nation's top sixty-five newspapers, and a Web browser search in November 1998 found 622,079 webpages mentioning Monica Lewinsky or Paula Jones.[21]

Toward Impeachment

When in doubt, tell the truth. It will confound your enemies and astound your friends.

Mark Twain

Between his testimony in the Paula Jones case on January 17, 1998, and his appearance before a grand jury on August 17, the president repeatedly denied, both publicly and privately, any contact with Lewinsky. The essentials of the scandal were in print within days of the first revelation. The president's efforts to delay or derail the independent counsel's investigation failed in July when Lewinsky agreed to testify in exchange for immunity. Facing overwhelming evidence against him, including physical evidence of an encounter, Clinton decided to testify before the grand jury on August 17 and spoke to the nation a few hours later. He admitted an "inappropriate relationship" and that he had misled people about it. However, throughout the looming impeachment process he would continue to give answers that were "evasive or nonresponsive rather than outright falsehoods."[22]

On September 9, 1998, the Starr Report was submitted to the House and immediately released to the public. Whatever facts it contained were quickly overlooked in favor of its graphic sexual descriptions. Each of the ten sexual encounters in the Oval Office was described in shocking detail, the 435-page report was put on the Internet, and juicy tidbits were soon broadcast. One observer called it "the most detailed pornographic government report in history." Press Secretary Mike McCurry was appalled that "all of the filters . . . in the world of journalism evaporated. . . ." Though there was a legal argument that the details of these intimacies were needed to refute the president's denial of a sexual relationship, it appeared to many to be an effort to undermine his public support and embarrass him into resigning.

The relationship between the White House and the press became increasingly adversarial, with enough blame to go around. McCurry, who maintained surprisingly cordial relations with reporters, resigned as press secretary in October, having been drained by the year's onslaught. During this period, Clinton usually appeared before the press only when a prestigious foreign leader was visiting, such as Nelson Mandela or Czech president Vaclav Havel. Their presence contrasted the newsmen's questions about the scandal with weighty issues of geopolitics. Presidential aides went over the heads of the press by appearing on a daily round of talk shows. By the opening of impeachment hearings before the House Judiciary Committee in November, more than 150 newspapers had called on the president to resign. Many in the press were befuddled that their saturation coverage of the sins of the chief executive had done so little to erode his high public approval.[23]

Despite the polls, and the mid-term elections—where the Democrats did better than expected—the Republican-dominated House voted on December 19, 1998, to impeach the president (which meant bringing charges to the Senate for trial). In coordinated statements, the White House and House Democratic leaders denounced "the politics of personal destruction." The president's public support reached a high point in the scandal right after the vote—73 percent. Another survey taken the next month after his 1999 State of the Union address, and in the midst of the Senate impeachment trial, showed that 77 percent approved of the speech. Mindful of this public support, the senators could not muster the two-thirds needed to convict and so, as expected, voted to acquit on February 12.

At the end stunned observers noted that "the atmosphere in Washington had been poisoned," that Republicans appeared "disoriented," Democrats "utterly reeled," and the nation was left "in a daze."[24] The public had moved on. While 2 million watched the Senate vote on CNN that night, twice as many were watching professional wrestling on a competing cable station.

The News of the Scandal, the Scandal of the News

A number of themes emerge from this scandal: some concern the public, some the president, and some the press.

The country's fascination with the Lewinsky scandal reflected the continuing cultural wars that have raged in the United States since the 1960s. For many conservatives, the president's adultery and lying symbolized the decline they saw overcoming the country. Now the decay had seeped into the very pinnacle of national authority. On the other side, liberals worried about the Puritanism and intolerance displayed by the right wing. They saw narrow-minded bigotry dressed up as morality. The media's exhaustive coverage only intensified this polarization.

Public opinion showed considerable stability in riding out the storm. The American people's ability to separate the public job of a president from his private life frustrated both camps. The public supported the job the president was doing, while disapproving of his personal failings and disbelieving his denials. Hardly reluctant to look at the lurid details, the public saw no reason why watching media entertainment should contaminate the tasks of governing. The dislike for politicians who exploited the scandal for partisan advantage, and the media who pandered to their increasing audience, may have reflected a general wish that elected officials return to the duties they were being paid to do. Clinton's skill showed in convincing the public that he at least wanted to get on with the tasks of his office.

The president was hardly an innocent, even beyond lying and adultery. From his arrival on the public stage, Clinton flourished in low-key informal settings. Avoiding the press he distrusted, Clinton went directly to the public, often through talk shows. But this media strategy combined with his seductive personality had turned the presidential image into something new. Howard Kurtz, media critic for the *Washington Post*, put it this way: "Bill Clinton dwelt in the same murky precincts of celebrity as Dennis Rodman, Courtney Love, and David Letterman. In a hundred-channel world the president had become just another piece of programming to be marketed. . . ."[25] From this view the exhaustive exposure given the scandal was a product of the president's

President Clinton demonstrates his sax appeal in a relaxed TV setting.
Reed Saxon/AP–Wide World Photos

celebrity status. Here was a "personal presidency" filled by a man with a compulsive desire to please audiences and a willingness to answer questions about what underwear he wore. As he lived by the talk show, so he would (almost) die by the talk shows. The price of personalizing his presidency was to weaken the press filters that made any aspects of his life off-limits.

The scandal revealed the limits of the media's impact. On one hand, the role of agenda-setting worked: Sex, lies, and tapes rose to the top of the country's list of compelling issues. The press had the nation thinking about the scandal, even if it was not able to tell the public *how* to think about it, that is, what frame to use to understand its significance. On the other hand, the flood of news had a diminishing effect which muted its impact on public opinion. By emphasizing sex to attract a large audience, the press may have made the story less politically relevant. Linking adultery to job performance seemed a stretch for most people. Defining the story as sex in the beginning may have minimized its relevance to governing in the end.[26] If the president's behavior didn't live up to the public's expectations, neither did it rise to the level of "high crimes and misdemeanors" required by the Constitution to remove him from office.

But there was a cost. It was paid in the coin of a chief executive distracted from the issues of world peace and domestic security that in a few years would tragically overtake the country. It was paid by his vice president, Al Gore, who failed to succeed to the presidency in part because he felt he needed to distance himself from the blemished administration he had served. It was paid in a public appalled and enthralled by the lurid chaos engulfing their government. And it was a price paid by a press that, while entertaining a larger audience, may have lost their respect by abandoning its mission as democracy's watchdog.

Notes

1. Kathleen Hall Jamieson and Paul Waldman, *The Press Effect* (New York: Oxford University Press, 2003), xiii.

2. Steven Brill, "Pressgate," in *Brill's Content*, August 1998. See also Mike Isikoff, *Uncovering Clinton: A Reporter's Story* (New York: Random House, 2000).

3. Ruth Marcus, "Starr: Relentless or Reluctant?" *Washington Post,* January 30, 1998.

4. As quoted by Ben H. Bagdikian, *The Media Monopoly,* 6th ed. (Boston: Beacon Press, 2000), xxiv.

5. Brill, "Pressgate." Much of this account of the early press coverage is taken from this extensive report used to launch Brill's media journal.

6. Brill, "Pressgate."

7. See John Anthony Maltese, "The Media: The New Media and the Lure of the Clinton Scandal," in Mark J. Rozell and Clyde Wilcox, eds., *The Clinton Scandal and the Future of American Government* (Washington, DC: Georgetown University Press, 2000).

8. See Larry J. Sabato, *Feeding Frenzy: Attack Journalism and American Politics* (Baltimore: Lanahan Publishers, 2000), 1.

9. The quote is from Brill, "Pressgate."

10. Maltese, 200.

11. Maltese, 200. Also see Howard Kurtz, *Spin Cycle* (New York: Touchstone, 1998), 307–308; and Joseph Hayden, *Covering Clinton* (Westport, CT: Praeger, 2002), Chapter 5.

12. Kurtz, Chapter 17.

13. Kurtz, 309–310.

14. Maltese, 205–206.

15. Sidney Blumenthal, *The Clinton Wars* (London: Penguin Books, 2003), 361.

16. W. Lance Bennett, *News: The Politics of Illusion,* 5th ed. (New York: Longman, 2003), 234

17. Molly W. Andolina and Clyde Wilcox, "Public Opinion: The Paradoxes of Clinton's Popularity," in Rozell and Wilcox, Chapter 9. For a critique of GOP willingness to ignore public opinion, see Lawrence Jacobs and Robert Y. Shapiro, *Politicians Don't Pander* (Chicago: University of Chicago Press, 2000), Chapter 9.

18. Andolina and Wilcox.

19. Jamieson is quoted by Bennett, 231.

20. Andolina and Wilcox, 188.

21. Doris A. Graber, *Mass Media and American Politics,* 6th ed. (Washington, DC: Congressional Quarterly Press, 2002), 316.

22. Richard A. Posner, *An Affair of State* (Cambridge, MA: Harvard University Press, 1999), 30.

23. Hayden, 91.

24. For an account of impeachment, see Peter Baker, *The Breach* (New York: Scribner, 2000).

25. Hayden, 96.

26. See Julie Yiortas and Ivana Segvic, "Revisiting the Clinton/Lewinsky Scandal: The Convergence of Agenda Setting and Framing," *Journalism & Mass Communication Quarterly* 80, no. 3 (Autumn 2003): 567–582.

chapter 10

Networking Congress

Passing Pension Reform

O n May 26, 2001, Congress passed President George W. Bush's first comprehensive tax cut. It was hailed as a major legislative victory. Included in the bill was a pension reform the *National Journal* described as "the only significant piece of the bill that wasn't part of Bush's original proposal."[1] Neither the administration nor most of both parties' legislative leadership had wanted pension reforms. That they ultimately were included was an accomplishment that reflected the power of a committed issue network.

Political scientists use "issue networks" to describe a community of policy experts and interests influencing a common subject. These experts may be in or out of government and may represent interest groups or members of Congress or think tanks. In the past they were called "iron triangles" or "subgovernments" and described as rigid, autonomous groups that operated to promote narrow policy goals unconnected to more democratic input. Contemporary issue networks are seen as ad hoc coalitions that are more flexible, more informal, more temporary, larger in size, and more open to new participants than the old iron triangles.[2]

Congress's passage of pension reform showed the importance of a retirement issue network and its mastery of the legislative process. The cooperation of the experts in the network, mostly congressional staffers and lobbyists, was essential at each stage of the legislation. In drawing up the bill, in plotting strategy, in exchanging intelligence, in lobbying members, in mobilizing grassroots contacts, and in compromising to pass the final bill, a small group made the difference. At the end, the divide between private lobbyists and public officials was easily bridged by their shared commitment to increasing retirement savings.

concepts highlighted

1. The independent role of Congress in modifying administration proposals is shown clearly in this case. Note that the new president engaged in **agenda setting** by introducing tax cuts, but then had to allow Congress to shape the final bill. In acting on pension reform, how did Congress reflect both its **governing** and **representation functions**?

2. The question of the **power of lobbyists** is an important one for political scientists. But the presence of a retirement issue network crossing public-private divisions suggests how difficult the question may be to answer in practice. What are some examples of private lobbyists dominating the network? When do government officials—elected and staff—seem to have the upper hand in the case? Would you expect to see this network operating in the recent debate over Social Security reform?

3. The **differences between how the House and Senate are organized** are illustrated in their contrasting treatment of the president's tax cuts. Note examples in the Senate where party unity was weak, individual senators voted independently, and staff were powerful. Did the decentralized Senate and its committees give the issue network's tactics more chance for success?

4. The struggle between Senate **party leaders and committee chairmen** played out around the tax cut legislation. How did the finance chairman use his **gatekeeping authority** in approving a bill to go to the floor to gain power for his committee? How did he and the issue network use bipartisanship to limit the influence of party leaders over the bill?

5. The **power of congressional staff** is best exercised quietly. Senate committee staffers are often considered the Hill's most powerful staff. Note how the Senate staffs used their issue expertise and network ties to influence the legislative process. Is it fair to consider them as part of the retirement issue network?

Following conventional wisdom for making an issue look popular, the room holding the press conference was too small for the crowd. Half of the eighty people had to stand against the walls of H137, the colonial-blue room on the House side of the U.S. Capitol. On this March 14, 2001, afternoon they had come for a press conference to hear two congressmen, Ohio Republican Rob Portman and Maryland Democrat Ben Cardin, launch a pension reform bill. Lining the table in the rear of the room were press releases from groups like the U.S. Chamber of Commerce, the brokerage firm Charles Schwab, the National Conference of State Legislatures, and the Securities Industry Association (SIA). Congressional staff and lobbyists, many talking to each other, outnumbered the press.

Congressman Portman led the pitch: Workers needed to save more for retirement; small businesses needed to expand their retirement plans; the plans needed to be simpler. On a day when the stock market was dropping 300 points, the Republican stressed that increased savings would "give our economy a needed boost" and bring stability to capital markets. He pointed out that the bill had 260 cosponsors, had passed the House overwhelmingly the previous session, and was endorsed by over 100 groups from labor to business. He was interrupted by applause when he mentioned that the bill was now called HR 10—a low number indicating House leadership support. (Whether the House was behind it enough to override partisan loyalties to the president and promises made to other tax cutting interests remained unclear.) Portman got knowing chuckles when he added that ten was a better number than 401.

Indeed. 401 was the number of House members who had voted for the bill the year before—an impressive demonstration of popularity. Except that it never became law, falling victim to election-year politics in the Senate. This year it was facing a new president's obstacles—President Bush's limit of $1.6 trillion in tax cuts, a ceiling that didn't include Portman-Cardin. Members were either pledging fidelity to the president or mumbling that taxes were already reduced too much. In a vote on the floor of either House, pension reform would pass. But would it get that far?

Saving for Retirement: Its History and Support

Portman-Cardin offered increased tax breaks to encourage increased retirement savings. It was the result of a four-year partnership by the two congressmen, committee hearings, and numerous studies by groups interested in the topic. The bill proposed increasing the limits on tax-deductible contributions to individual retirement accounts (IRAs) from $2,000 to $5,000, increasing the amount that could be contributed to employees' 401(k)s and other pension plans, and making it easier for workers to take their pensions with them when they switched jobs. The existing contribution limits were twenty years old, and inflation had eroded much of their value. Supporters pointed to studies showing that Americans were saving less and less, and that one-quarter of the population had less than $10,000 saved for retirement.

A similar bill was introduced in the Senate (S 742) by Finance Committee Chairman Charles E. Grassley (R-Iowa) and the panel's chief Democrat, Max Baucus of Montana. The Senate bill added tax credits for low-income taxpayers, cash paybacks for those whose incomes were too low to benefit from reducing their taxes. The Democrats had pushed these tax credits into the Senate bill but had failed to add them in the House. This resulted in the Senate bill costing $30 billion more than the estimated $50 billion (over ten years) of the House proposal.

These bills were the product of an evolution in thinking about how Americans would pay for retirement. Traditionally there had been a defined benefit plan by which workers would get a fixed pension when they retired, based on their salary and years employed. Under President Ronald Reagan, the Treasury Department issued regulations allowing for contributions for retirement to be tax deductible under 401(k) of the code. This encouraged businesses to reduce their pension obligations and turn over responsibility for them to employees. Republicans liked retirement contributions as a way to get workers to invest in the stock market and support investors on issues like lower taxes. The plans grew rapidly in popularity, paralleling the profitable stock markets of the 1980s and 1990s. In 1984 there were $92 billion in 401(k) plans. By 1999, the figure stood at $1.7 trillion in 401(k)s, and another 50 million workers held $2.5 trillion in personal retirement accounts.[3]

Beyond the benefits to Republican political goals, a host of economic interests gained from changing from fixed pensions to individual accounts. First were the providers of financial services, securities firms like Charles Schwab and Merrill Lynch who could appeal to new customers wishing to save for retirement by investing in stocks and mutual funds. Many modest-income families entered the stock market for the first time. Business opportunities expanded for life insurers, retirement plan providers, and various financial services. Their members' involvement in these accounts drew the support of labor unions, ranging from police to bricklayers, and nonprofit groups, such as the Association of American Universities and the National League of Cities.

These interests were represented in Washington by their own offices, by trade associations, and by many specialized groups that arose to monitor and lobby for retirement issues. The Securities Industry Association representing "Wall Street" (or, more precisely, the investment brokers trading in the stock market) was active in pension reform, with member firms aiming at individual customers such as Fidelity and Edward Jones most involved in the lobbying. The Profit Sharing Council of America (PSCA) represented employers providing plans for their employees; the American Benefits Council had hundreds of large American businesses that sponsored plans. Several umbrella structures, with overlapping members, chaired meetings for plotting strategy for the bill: The Savings Coalition focused on IRAs, the Retirement Savings Network's members were trade associations of plan sponsors and providers, and the Financial Services Roundtable included banks and insurers.

One group notably absent from this coalition was the AARP (American Association of Retired Persons), arguably the most powerful lobby in Washington. This national membership organization of seniors was a supporter of traditional pensions and had avoided proposals undermining these plans. Many meetings with other groups and Hill representatives would be needed before they would support the legislation. Removing their opposition would prove crucial in the May victories in the Senate.[4]

It should not be assumed that private groups were the driving force behind the reform. In addition to Congressmen Portman and Cardin, active House members included Earl Pomeroy (D–N.D.), Majority Leader Dick Armey (R–Tex.), and several committee staff members from the Ways and Means Committee. On the Senate side the moderate partnership of Grassley-Baucus, would be central. Paralleling this was the longstanding involvement by the Senate Finance Committee staff on retirement issues. In pulling the bill through the Senate, the staff would provide day-to-day management, orchestrate the lobbying, and suggest needed modifications. Their ties to lobbyists, nearly all of whom had worked on the Hill on this issue, were critical. Shared experiences not only led to a similarity of outlook, but it also gave the issue network a formidable vantage point for knowing what arguments would work, which lobbyists members would listen to, and which members/staff were critical in gaining victory.[5]

The Early Rounds of Retirement Reform

This retirement issue network began the new Congress on a cautionary note— none of its strengths had been sufficient the year before. It had seemed that 2000 would be the year when pension reform would become law. The bill as HR 1102 passed the House twice overwhelmingly. Arriving in the Senate, it was passed unanimously by the Finance Committee and had ninety-five Senators signed on as cosponsors. Members of the Clinton administration voiced support, editorial comment was favorable, and public opinion was positive.

Yet the bill never came to a vote in the Senate. Election-year politics were the main reason the Republican leadership kept it off the floor. As one Republican lobbyist put it, "Why should they have to negotiate with Bill Clinton on these tax cuts and then watch him take credit for whatever passes?" The leadership also hoped for a GOP administration in 2001, when pension reform could be part of a Republican tax cut.

The leadership was not feeling much pressure in 2000 to pass the bill. The intense push of an organized campaign was lacking. One lobbyist described support as "a mile wide and an inch thick." Caught in the political undertow of an election year, the lobbyists were reluctant to fire up a broad grassroots campaign to challenge the Republican leaders, who were traditional allies of the business community. Grassroots was a way of enhancing Washington relationships, not undermining them. Until the very end, GOP leaders promised their support—and never delivered it. As the president of one trade association grimly concluded, "In Washington you get screwed by your friends."

Based on the 2000 experience, the House (where the Constitution requires tax legislation to start) was not expected to be a problem. House Speaker

Dennis Hastert (R–Ill.) had backed Portman-Cardin in the last Congress. Majority Leader Dick Armey was a strong advocate of individual retirement accounts, believing they involved the working class in conservative economic policies. The chairman of the Ways and Means Committee, which is in charge of taxes, had repeatedly sponsored expanded IRAs and had helped steer the previous pension bill through the House.

These expectations for a smooth House passage were borne out. Despite not being part of the president's tax bill, pension reform passed overwhelmingly in a 407-24 vote on May 2. Democratic efforts to liberalize parts of the bill to help poor people with tax credits were beaten. The administration, facing steep odds, didn't oppose reform as a separate bill. The Senate would be where the critical battle over including pension reform in the tax package would take place.

In the Senate, the Grassley-Baucus Retirement Savings and Security Act of 2001 was introduced on April 6 with fifteen cosponsors and muted publicity. This was virtually the same bill that the Finance Committee had passed unanimously in the previous year and that the Senate leadership had refused to allow on the floor. Jim Delaplane of the American Benefits Council and a former legislative counsel put reform's chances at below 50 percent. Ex-Senate staffer Liz Liess of the Securities Industry Association agreed. The Senate had already lowered the president's tax cut target from $1.6 to $1.35 trillion—hardly reassuring to those interests waiting to be included in the bill. With neither party highlighting retirement reform, the chances of adding $50 billion of costs to the tax cut slid further away.[6]

Senate Grassroots

The initial efforts of the network groups focused on getting enough Senate cosponsors to pressure the leadership to act. Through lobbying, advertising, and grassroots activities, a message was delivered: The savings rate had fallen to the lowest level since the Great Depression, resulting in a "retirement crisis" for baby boomers. Raising the 1981 limits on IRAs and 401(k) plans would revive savings. And these savings were vital for increasing investments to fuel the nation's economic growth.[7]

Throughout the first months of 2001, the issue network encouraged grassroots contacts from the key states of the members of the Senate Finance Committee. The Savings Coalition listed some 100 town hall meetings in the states of twenty-nine senators and gathered reports from Coalition members who attended. These were usually employees of local brokerages who asked the targeted senator his position on retirement legislation. The most extensive listing of town hall meetings was for Chairman Grassley with sixteen meetings over four days in April.

Who
CARES
About
RETIREMENT
Security?

Our own Senator Chuck Grassley cares about retirement security. He has introduced the Retirement Security and Savings Act of 2001 to make it easier for Americans to save for retirement.

The bill will raise the amount of money Americans can set aside for retirement in their IRA or other retirement plans. And it contains additional benefits for small business employees, working mothers, and those nearing retirement.

Today, Americans worry that they will not have enough for retirement. That's why the Retirement Security and Savings Act is an essential investment in every American's retirement security.

Introducing this bill is an important first step. But Senator Grassley needs to hear from you that retirement security is a priority. So, call Senator Grassley's Des Moines office, (515) 284-4890, thank him for introducing the Retirement Security and Savings Act of 2001, and urge him to make sure the bill becomes law this year.

Because retirement security should be part of ever American's future.

Call Senator Grassley's Des Moines office at (515) 284-4890

Paid for by
THE SAVINGS
COALITION
OF AMERICA

For more information, visit www.savingscoalition.org

This ad was run in Iowa in support of retirement reform. Note that it supports Senator Grassley while asking Iowans to phone his local office to communicate grassroots urgency behind the issue.
Courtesy The Savings Coalition of America

A website was set up, *PassPensionReform.org,* to prepare a national petition in favor of legislation "to expand retirement savings this year." Firms used the website to encourage employees and customers to write their Congress members through the website. The results were 12,000 signatures on the petition going to the Hill. One lobbyist considered the website "completely ineffective," reflecting the network's leaders' desire to keep their members active in the campaign, despite the questionable impact.

Mailings were sent out and calls were made. Bonner & Associates, a Washington grassroots firm, was hired in May to phone locally prominent leaders of business, unions, and other groups to communicate with their senators. Crucial moderate Democrats on the Senate Finance Committee were targeted for CEO calls, visits to state offices from stockbrokers who were fundraisers, ads running in *USA Today* on May 7 and 8, and radio commercials in Arkansas,

Louisiana, Iowa, and Montana. Some timely visits occurred by accident. Edward Jones, a national brokerage, was holding product-training sessions in Washington on May 8 and 9. The Savings Coalition took advantage of the hundreds of agents and employees in town during this critical week. Teams were organized, given talking points, and dispatched to their senators' offices accompanied by Washington lobbyists. They asked their senator to sponsor the pension bill, to include it in the tax cut, and to speak to Grassley. Eighty-six meetings were held, all with Senate staff. The response was reported to be favorable.

With few exceptions, the grassroots input came from providers, not beneficiaries, of retirement programs. Attendance at meetings, letters, phone calls, use of the website, and visits to Washington were from the employees of the industry that provided retirement services. The strength of the issue network reflected the groups that derived benefits from the legislation and had the resources for a full-court lobbying effort. Though the industry boasted that 50 million Americans were affected by the bill, the rewards were either too diffused or not sufficient to mobilize the beneficiaries.[8]

A grassroots campaign involved costs, and not only in the money spent. Many in the financial services industry were reluctant to use their clients for grassroots pressure. They thought that asking customers—in the monthly mailing of account information—to write their congressmen appeared self-serving and outside the boundaries of a proper financial relationship. Such pressure could lead to unwanted press attention.[9] Another danger from an extensive campaign was put simply by one leader of a trade association: "The lobbyists were afraid they'd lose. If they had spent too much money on grassroots and then they had lost, they would be exposed to criticism by the groups putting up the funds." Less money, less risk.[10]

The network's goal in grassroots lobbying was not to change minds, since almost everyone in Congress favored reform. Instead, according to one lobbyist, these actions were designed "to raise the fervor for the issue." According to an involved staffer, "grassroots got people to pay attention to it." And the grassroots input that meant the most came when influential voters personally contacted their member of Congress.[11]

Several Days in May

Once begin the dance of legislation, and you must struggle through its mazes as best you can to the breathless end—if any end there be.

President Woodrow Wilson

A complicated legislative dance faced the reformers in the Senate. Not only were the leaders of the two parties clashing with each other over the tax bill, they were both fighting with the Finance Committee over who would oversee the needed compromises. The administration was trying to retain as much of their original tax bill as possible, while reassuring the many business interests left out and avoiding the fights over who would be included. And these multiple conflicts were occurring within a budget process with complex deadlines, imposed dollar limits, and varied legislative majorities. Simply understanding the budget process required a rare expertise.

The Senate strategy of the retirement network was to convince a few key moderates to make their support for the tax bill conditional on retirement reforms being added. The strategy focused on getting four Democratic senators on the Finance Committee to press Chairman Grassley to include retirement in the tax bill he was writing. In this strategy, the network's goals overlapped with the chairman's. He needed those Democratic votes to win a majority of his committee behind his version of tax reform, called the "Chairman's Markup." His gatekeeping authority was sufficient to keep the bill from going to the Senate floor for a vote. As long as pensions were in the bill, the network wanted to help him get his majority for the Markup, which would become the vehicle for the tax bill passing the Senate.

As the Senate negotiations heated up in early May, the administration made clear it was happy with the House bill. However, with a 50/50 party split in the Senate, and Democrats pushing for smaller tax cuts, the best the president could get was a compromise budget resolution setting a total cost of the tax package at $1.35 trillion. This umbrella figure under which the tax cuts had to fit limited the administration's ability to lower income tax rates. (The House proposals totaled $1.64 trillion.) Both punishments and promises were dangled before supporters to keep pensions out of the bill. A White House lobbyist pointedly told a Merrill Lynch executive that the president didn't want retirement in his tax package, and reminded him that his firm had other fish to fry with the new administration. The White House promised a second tax bill the next year containing pension reform—along with other left-behind tax cuts. Most in the network thought verbal pledges of future help were, in the words of Hollywood tycoon Sam Goldwyn, not worth the paper they were written on.

But the major line of tension was not with the administration, it was with the Senate Finance Committee. Republican Senator Grassley had recently become chairman of the committee and was determined to restore its power, which had been whittled away in recent years by his own party leaders. To oppose his party infringing on his committee's power, Chairman Grassley joined with Democrats to resist. Working with Max Baucus, the senior Democrat on the committee, the chairman drafted a tax plan of his own that could win bipartisan support. In doing this, he faced opposition from GOP leaders who wanted more cuts and Democratic leaders who wanted fewer. He also faced a budget deadline of mid-May, after which the tax bill would no longer be protected from amendments under special budget-reconciliation rules.[12]

Despite supporting pension reform, Grassley was at first unwilling to embrace the measure as part of his Markup. The chairman was looking for a committee majority and he was unwilling to allow any new tax cuts into his bill without getting full commitments of support from the members who wanted them. The chairman's reluctance was also a shrewd way to motivate the pension network to push his committee to support Markup. In a May 3 meeting with twenty-five pension supporters, he was noncommittal about whether he could include their provisions. He said he wanted to talk to other committee members—an invitation to those attending to continue lobbying them. He upped the pressure by telling the press afterward that he was having difficulty finding room for retirement in his draft.[13]

Behind the scenes the chairman was reaching different conclusions in meetings with his committee. On the morning of May 3, before he met with the pension lobbyists, he had met alone with Baucus. They had concluded that to get a majority behind the tax bill they needed pensions. The argument that Baucus brought with him was the one the chairman needed to convince his own party leadership. Baucus held four Democratic votes—including his own—that gave the tax bill a majority on the committee (one Republican had opposed the tax cuts). These moderate Democrats would oppose their party in voting for both pension reform and the Chairman's Markup.

The network's strategy reinforced the chairman by targeting these centrist Democrats on the Finance Committee. Three of them—John B. Breaux of Louisiana, Blanche Lincoln of Arkansas, and Robert Torricelli of New Jersey—had joined Baucus—against their party—in voting for the budget resolution and later for both pension reform and the tax bill. These votes were crucial for the majority the chairman needed and didn't have.

But there was a price to the network for including pension reform in the Markup. Staffers from Senate Finance met with industry representatives at 2 p.m. on Friday, May 4. It was a good news, bad news session. The staff was more optimistic about pension reform prospects than the chairman had been the day before. But for the first time the figure of $40 billion was floated. This figure was reached by reducing the amounts of retirement savings allowed a tax deduction (say from $5,000 to $3,000) and by pushing back the year the deductions would go into effect. The reaction was grumbling in the industry. The staff made clear that part of the new reduced figure would go to credits for low-income taxpayers, which was important for keeping Democratic support. The industry, not seeing much business coming from poor families and knowing the credits used up money for tax cuts, was at best indifferent. The staff insisted the credits remain.

This threat from committee Democrats was not an idle one. By the network's count, Grassley had eight votes of twenty members of his committee for

The "dance of legislation" involves talking, talking, and more talking.
© Ashe/Folio, Inc.

the bill, without Baucus and his Democratic allies. With the retirement provisions added, the four centrist Democrats allowed the Chairman's Markup to pass. There were, of course, other factors in play for these senators, including election politics. All of their states, except New Jersey, had voted for Bush in 2000. Baucus's Montana was overwhelmingly Republican and the Democratic senator was up for reelection the next year.[14]

On May 11 Grassley and Baucus released a jointly drafted outline of the Chairman's Markup with a total of $1.35 trillion in tax cuts over ten years. Their bipartisan proposal was roundly attacked by the leaders of both parties, the GOP for departing from the president's proposal and the Democrats for giving in to most of the tax cuts. Because their Senate allies needed Grassley's support to pass the tax cut on the floor, the White House response was muted. In private the Senate GOP leaders had already conceded to the chairman—at least, to get the bill through the Senate and to the conference committee of both houses where they saw more opportunity to remove objectionable parts, including pensions. For now, with a solid moderate majority in favor, retirement remained in the bill. A week after approval by the Finance Committee, the bill passed the Senate.[15]

Behind the Scenes with the Senate Staff

Throughout the process, the congressional staff helped in knitting together the intricate legislative tapestry. While these staffers worked for their Senate bosses, they played key roles as both advocates of retirement reform and managers of the legislative process. At times this led them to offer guidance to the lobbyists, including advice on how best to influence the senators on the committee that employed them.[16]

The key Senate staffers (Maria Friese and Diann Howland) had worked on the retirement issue for years. Respected in the retirement community as knowledgeable and energetic, they, in the words of one lobbyist, had "as much at stake in getting the bill done as anyone on the outside." In meetings with network members, they acted to coordinate the groups' efforts, informed them of the state of play of the legislation, and focused lobbying activities. Staff and lobbyists exchanged gossip on what the Senate offices were saying about retirement and the overall tax cut. Staff commented on what arguments were helpful, which senators should be targeted, and what was legislatively possible. The closeness of the cooperation with the staff was illustrated when a lobbyist for a securities firm asked Diann Howland, Senator Grassley's pension staffer, whether the ads in Iowa were helping or hurting. "Keep doing what you're doing," she replied.

The Senate staff members were not just acting on behalf of their bosses. They were committed supporters of retirement who had been promoting the issue for years. As a former staffer who is a current lobbyist put it, "Staff work on Capitol Hill not to help a member but to get something done." Staff wanted a bill enacted—a bill that had repeatedly come close to passing. This did not mean they were loose cannons operating outside their bosses' interests. But both their autonomy and their involvement as retirement supporters in pushing the legislation were evident at each stage.

Staff meetings with lobbyists served a number of purposes. For ease of scheduling, it was more cost effective to have one meeting with all the lobbyists rather than individual meetings with the separate groups. Meeting together also encouraged the network to stick together and not to target specific provisions at the expense of the overall bill. Questions asked and answered at these meetings included: Where are we on cosponsors? What do these senators need to be brought on board? What should the groups' next efforts be?

An example of how the staff operated was an April 24 meeting called by the Senate Finance staffers for Grassley and Baucus. Attending were key retirement lobbyists, including the Savings Coalition, and individual company's representatives such as Merrill Lynch and AARP. The lobbyists were told to get senators on Finance to call Baucus and Grassley and ask them to include the retirement provisions in the bill. That committee staffers could recommend strategies for interest groups to lobby their bosses seems more curious to outsiders than to those involved. The staffers were operating within the chairman's policy agenda. He needed to have the support of his committee members to include retirement. He needed them to commit to this priority so that he could convince his party's leadership that these provisions were needed to pass the tax bill. The staff was using the lobbyists, and vice versa.

Conclusions

Many in the network expected the retirement provisions to be jettisoned during the conference committee. But Senate moderates held firm. Helping the moderates was the announcement that Vermont senator James Jeffords was leaving the GOP, giving Democrats a Senate majority. This surprise switch disheartened the Republican leadership and undermined their promises of a future tax bill. It cemented a tax cut close to the Senate version. Pension reform stayed in as the Senate moved on to deal with its unique mid-year change in party control. The timing was right, and fortune smiled.[17]

A few lessons can be drawn from this success story. Both bipartisanship and expertise were critical. Despite the headlines of nasty partisanship darkening the corridors of the Capitol, this case echoes with bipartisan cooperation. In the drafting of the bills, in acquiring cosponsors, in targeting lobbyists, and in grassroots efforts, bipartisanship was central. Pension reform was positioned in the Senate as a victory for the moderates, reflecting the broad coalition of private and public interests pushing the reforms. Expertise also counted. The players in this issue network were among those best informed on the bill's substance and the legislative procedures. Once these experts were in the pension reform coalition, their party or public/private status mattered less than what information, skills, or resources they brought with them. The players in the network had similar professional backgrounds on the Hill, a shared commitment to retirement reform, and an immediate need for pragmatic policymaking.

The collaboration between staffers and lobbyists was central. Accurate information for targeting officials and timing the lobbying could only come from insiders on the Hill. The network's lobbying/grassroots campaign in part directed by congressional staff was critical. Retirement reform had not lacked an overwhelming majority in the past. What the reform needed was *intensity* from a few well-placed members making it a priority. This meant gaining moderates on the Senate Finance Committee to condition their support of the tax bill on including pension reform. That, not a roll call majority, was key.

The grassroots campaign was a reminder that retirement measures conferred important benefits on 50 million people. The outside-the-Beltway efforts kept the issue in front of the Congress. But these phone calls, e-mails, and visits were not a result of a popular national response. They were joined at the hip with

and directed by the providers of retirement services, rather than their con-
sumers. Grassroots input was less a reflection of public opinion than of a strategy by a Washington-based network.

In focusing on the politics of the legislative process, it is easy to overlook the
substance of the issue. Retirement linked to savings was of national importance. Its connection with the stock market, the aging of the baby boomer generation, and financial security were part of a media buzz. As one lobbyist said,
"We were on the right side of a needed popular issue." Its political maturity
was also linked to the work that the network members had done to publicize
it.[18] It had popular and political support from its past defeats. By 2001 there
was a sense of inevitability around its eventual passage: a question not of whether
but of when.

Despite this ripeness, the legislative outcome was unpredictable. Even after
the House passage, questions remained whether pension reform would be included in the Chairman's Markup, whether it would survive a committee vote,
whether it would stay in the conference committee report, and whether the
coalition would hold together. Even the most savvy participants voiced dark
prophecies at various times on the outcome.

Passing major legislation in Congress seems complex, confusing, and uncertain, because it is complex, confusing, and uncertain.

*It was another crowded room in Washington. This time it was a bar, Gordon Biersch
Restaurant, a few blocks from Capitol Hill where the people who had, as the announcement read, "survived" pension reform gathered to celebrate. Lobbyists and staff—
mostly thirty-somethings—showed up with a few congressmen, including Portman and
Cardin. The party was a bit too casual to expect a senator.*

*Although alcohol was being liberally consumed, the party was fairly subdued, per-
haps because it was now late June, one month after the tax bill had passed, and their
accomplishment was old news. Some in the room were preparing to deal with Treasury
on the rules for implementing the legislation, an effort that many thought equally
important to passing the bill. Others, including the congressmen, were talking about
further changes needed in retirement plans. By 9 in the evening, the party was pretty
much over. It was a weeknight, and people had to go to work the next day.*

Notes

1. John Maggs, "And You Thought 401(k)s Were a Safe Bet," *National Journal,* July 7,
   2001, 2178.
2. For a description and history of the term, see Jeffrey M. Berry, *The Interest Group
   Society,* 3rd ed. (New York: Longman, 1997), Chapter 9, "The Rise of Issue Networks."

Also see Robert H. Salisbury et al., "Triangles, Networks, and Hollow Cores: The Complex Geometry of Washington Interest Representation," in Mark P. Petracca, *The Politics of Interests* (Boulder, CO: Westview Press, 1992), 130–149.

3. The degree that this change in pensions pressured workers into the stock market and served conservative political goals has not received wide comment. See Richard Nadler, "A Direct Contribution," *National Review Online, nationalreview.com,* May 7, 2001; and Nadler, "The Rise of Worker Capitalism," *Policy Analysis* (Washington, DC: Cato Institute, November 1, 1999).

4. Letter, Horace B. Deets, Executive Director of AARP, to Senator Charles Grassley, April 2, 2001.

5. What follows is based on the author's research done at the time the tax cut legislation was moving through Congress between March and July 2001. I interviewed two dozen participants in the lobbying campaign, attended strategy meetings of the groups, and was given access to a considerable number of their memos and reports.

6. Interviews, James M. Delaplane, Jr., American Benefits Council Offices, April, 5, 2001; Liz Liess, Securities Industry Association Offices, March 9, 2001.

7. See Charles R. Schwab, "How Congress Can Stop a US Retirement Crisis," *Bridge-News,* April 10, 2001.

8. One study of an early version of the bill found that the bottom 60 percent of the population would receive only 4 percent of the benefits from the pension reforms. See Peter R. Orszag et al., "House-Passed Pension Changes Would Overwhelmingly Benefit Corporate Executives and Owners," Center on Budget and Policy Priorities, August 1, 2000.

9. Interview, Bill DeReutter, Merrill Lynch Offices, Willard, March 22, 2001.

10. Interviews, Kathy Hamor, The Savings Coalition, June 4, 2001; Steve Judge, Securities Industry Association, May 2, 2001.

11. An interesting discussion of how lobbyists decide on tactics to use to influence congressional committees can be found in Marie Hognacki and David C. Kimball, "The Who and How of Organizations' Lobbying Strategies in Committee," *The Journal of Politics* 61, no. 4 (November 1999): 999–1024.

12. "Grassley-Baucus Tax Blueprint Heads for Rough-and-Tumble Markup," *CQ Weekly,* May 12, 2001, 1069–1070.

13. "House Retirement Measure Unlikely to Gain a Place in Senate Tax Package," *CQ Weekly,* May 5, 2001, 1004.

14. From lobbyist interviews.

15. Lori Nitschke, "Senate Tax Bill Trade-Offs Leave a Fragile Coalition," *CQ Weekly,* May 19, 2001, 1145–1149.

16. This inside-outside coordination between legislators and lobbyists, though without the emphasis on the role of staff, is well presented in Scott H. Ainsworth, "The Role of Legislators in the Determination of Interest Group Influence," *Legislative Studies Quarterly* XXII, no. 4 (November 1997): 517–533.

17. See Lori Nitschke, "Tax Cut Deal Reached Quickly as Appetite for Battle Fades," *CQ Weekly,* May 26, 2001, 1251–1255.

18. An example of which is Marc Lackritz, "Raise Contribution Limits on 401(k)s, IRAs Now," *Houston Chronicle,* April 23, 2001.

chapter 11

9/11

Presidential Power in a Crisis

I n his classic essay "The Two Presidencies," noted political scientist Aaron Wildavsky divides the chief executive in half. He contrasts the wide powers a president has in directing national security policies with the severe limits a president faces in trying to shape domestic affairs. Wildavsky argues that the overwhelming power a chief executive has in foreign and military matters compared to his restrained influence domestically, especially in dealing with Congress, creates almost separate presidencies. The checks and balances in our federal system means that only in a time of an extraordinary crisis, such as Franklin D. Roosevelt faced in the 1930s Great Depression, can a president succeed in dominating domestic policy. Yet, Wildavsky says, "Serious setbacks to the president in controlling foreign policy are extraordinary and unusual."[1]

In the following case, President George W. Bush confronted both the challenges and the opportunities set in motion by the terrorist attacks on September 11, 2001. The resulting national security crisis gave the president a unique, if temporary, dominance over the political system as well as unquestioned national leadership. These first attacks on American soil since Pearl Harbor concentrated government policymaking in the hands of a wartime commander-in-chief. How he used the powers of his office, for both foreign and domestic policies, to rally public opinion behind him and to direct the government's response marked the weeks immediately following the attacks. As the crisis faded, the limits to presidential power became increasingly visible. Supporting these restraints were rival institutions, such as Congress, the opposition Democrats, the media, and interest groups, all of whom had priorities and perspectives different from the chief executive.

concepts highlighted

1. The president, as chief of state, is often portrayed as a **symbol of national unity**. Filling the top political office elected by the entire country, he represents the nation in many rituals that in other countries are reserved to royalty. How did the president in this crisis use his symbolic role to rally the country at the disaster sites, in religious ceremonies, and in public speeches? What impact did this symbolic role have on the president's political power?

2. The individual **personality of a president** is part of executive power. Note the incidents when President Bush acted in a way that reflected his own energy and inclinations—his first tentative reactions to the attacks, the creation of the so-called Bush Doctrine, the assertion of his authority over crisis decision-making, and his emotional reaction to the tragedy.

3. While he was publicly rallying the nation, the president was carrying out his **roles as chief executive and commander-in-chief**. Look for examples of President Bush managing the bureaucracy by choosing a lead agency for the invasion of Afghanistan or by selecting a military strategy. Did his refusal to blame anyone in government for the 9/11 disasters reflect a chief executive protecting subordinates he depended on?

4. The **president's influence over media** during the crisis was impressive. How did the president simplify and focus media coverage of 9/11 and the government's response? How did press framing of 9/11 reflect the government's priorities? Was the media acting independently or was it reflecting a national consensus?

5. **Bipartisan congressional deference to the executive** was apparent in this crisis, but was neither permanent nor complete. How did Congress cooperate with the president, from leadership meetings to congressional resolutions? How did Congress assert its independence, from "sunset" provisions in the USA Patriot Act to federalizing airport security?

On Tuesday morning, September 11, 2001, four teams of nineteen Arab terrorists took control of four California-bound jets shortly after they left three East Coast airports. Using the planes as "smart bombs," they crashed into both towers of the World Trade Center and the Pentagon. (The fourth plane, apparently thwarted by passengers, crashed into a field in Pennsylvania.) New York's huge 110-story towers collapsed to the ground, killing some three thousand people, while almost three hundred were killed at the Pentagon. A stunned nation watched the doomsday images on television, over and over.

The national reaction dramatized the sense of panic. Immediately after the planes hit, all commercial aviation was grounded and the nation's airports were closed. Employees were ordered out of the U.S. Capitol and White House. As rumors of further attacks spread, landmarks such as Disneyland, Mount Rushmore, and the Seattle

Stunned New Yorkers watched as the World Trade Towers burned.
© Reuters/Corbis

Space Needle were evacuated. All three stock exchanges shut down for the week. Major League Baseball called off its games, marking the first time since World War I that a national emergency had canceled three days of games. Americans worried that September 11 might be just the beginning of horrors to come.

The First Hours

"On September 10, 2001, George Bush was not on his way to a very successful presidency." These words, written by a former Bush speechwriter, were not far off the mark. The economy was slumping and corporate scandals filled the headlines, as did stories of the president's laid-back work habits. Memories of the embittered 2000 election remained fresh in many minds. Bush's approval rating stood at 51 percent in early September, lower than any president after eight months in office, except for Gerald Ford, whose popularity suffered after his pardon of Richard Nixon.

Following 9/11, both public and political opinion instinctively looked to the president. As chief of state he embodied the nation, but his role did not stop at symbols. He was also expected to define the enemy, to set out a course of action for the country, and, understandably, to provide reassurance. Underlying President Bush's initial actions lay a whispered doubt: Was this commander-in-chief—barely eight months in office, elected by a minority of voters, and with almost no foreign policy experience—up to the job? A *New York Times* editorial bluntly declared that the president "remains an untested figure." (A year earlier, the electorate had been divided over candidate Bush's ability to deal with an international crisis: 45 percent thought he could; 46 percent were uneasy.)[2]

The first hours of the crisis were not reassuring to those with doubts about the personal character of the new chief executive. For starters, it took the president most of the day just to get to the office.

His morning had begun in an elementary school in Sarasota, Florida, where he was plugging his education reform, No Child Left Behind. When he first got news of the attacks, he continued reading to a class of students and then took twelve hours to return to the White House. His appearance afterward was described as "tentative, tense, and shocked."[3] Because of security fears, Air Force One had taken a zigzag course returning to Washington, first to an air base near Shreveport, Louisiana, and then to a command post in Omaha, Nebraska, where Bush conducted a meeting of the National Security Council by videophone to Washington. While the Secret Service worried that the attacks hadn't ended yet, the president's political aides had to face another issue: How could President Bush communicate control and confidence to the nation from a bunker in Nebraska? Or, as a *USA Today* reporter noted, "Not since the British burned the White House in 1814 has a President been persuaded by security concerns to avoid the capital."[4]

Arriving back at the White House that night, President Bush gave a brief talk from the Oval Office. A "somber" chief executive sitting alone at his desk assured the 80 million people watching that "Our country is strong. . . . Terrorist acts can shake the foundation of our biggest buildings, but they cannot touch the foundation of America." He declared that the government would continue "without interruption," that the search was underway to find those behind the evil acts, and that both allies and members of Congress would stand together to win the war against terrorism. He ended by asking for prayers for those who grieved and promised, "America has stood down enemies before, and we will do so this time."

A President's Public Response

The general public is much more dependent on presidents in foreign affairs than in domestic matters.

Aaron Wildavsky

In the coming days, the president expanded on these themes. He was shown offering support to victims and rescuers, demonstrating national unity, defining an unseen enemy, and executing a strong military response. His major audiences at home were the American public and Congress. And he moved skillfully to gain the support of both.

Congress was reminded of its physical dependency on the executive in a graphic way. Unlike the executive branch, Congress had no evacuation plan on September 11. Members of Congress wandered around, prayed with the chaplain, or went home. Rumors circulated of more planes heading to Washington. Vice-President Dick Cheney ordered that the leaders of Congress be taken to a secure location (rumored to be in West Virginia). When, later, one Republican senator demanded in a phone call to Cheney that the leadership be returned to Washington so that Congress could convene, the vice-president refused. The senator pointed out that Congress was an independent branch of government not under executive control. Cheney replied, "We control the helicopters."[5]

On his first full day back in the White House after the attacks, the president used the national attention focused on him to define the challenge and position himself leading the nation's response. He escalated his language, calling the attacks "more than acts of terror; they were acts of war," thus laying the foundation for military action. News reports showed him calling leaders of Britain, France, Germany, Russia, and China. His press secretary described the president as "rallying an international coalition to combat terrorism." He was photographed meeting with his security advisors and then with congressional leaders on new defense spending. The House passed a resolution of support, and Secretary of State Colin Powell sent stern public messages to other countries: "You're either with us or against us."

As the week went on, George Bush demonstrated the power of the presidency as both a single human being and a branch of government. In a way that only an individual chief executive could do, he personally connected to the range of feelings washing over Americans, from sadness to anger. He comforted victims, thanked rescue workers at the Pentagon and at the World Trade Center site, and reflected the nation's raw wounds. Two days after the attacks, when he got off the phone after talking with New York mayor Rudolph Giuliani, a reporter described him this way: "The president's eyes glistened with emotion as he blinked to hold back tears. 'I'm a loving guy,' he said. 'And

This picture of the president with a firefighter by his side at the site of the destroyed Towers became a symbol for a rallying nation.
Paul J. Richards/AFP/Getty Images

I'm also someone, however, who's got a job to do and I intend to do it. And this is a terrible moment.'"[6]

A president has been described as a "democratic priest-king," and this religious image was apparent in much of what Bush did that first week.[7] When he declared a national "day of prayers and remembrance," his proclamation read, ". . . in the face of all this evil, we remain strong and united, one nation under God." During a televised service at Washington Cathedral on September 14, Bush said, "The commitment of our fathers is now the calling of our time. We ask almighty God to watch over our nation and grant us patience and resolve in all that is to come."

The president was also the commander-in-chief, rallying the country for what lay ahead. In that same cathedral service, Bush talked tough: "This conflict was begun on the timing and terms of others; it will end in a way and at an hour of our choosing." Two days after the attack, the president declared, "The nation must understand this is now the focus of my administration."

In the coming days, the president pointedly did *not* do certain things. As head of the executive branch, he publicly demonstrated loyalty to those under him by not blaming anyone in the government for not anticipating the attack. Although the hijackings represented an enormous intelligence failure, the president showed his confidence in the CIA by being photographed meeting with its director. Bush also tried to separate the terrorists from the religion they claimed to represent. He posed at a meeting with American Islamic leaders, declaring that the hijackers had nothing to do with peaceful Muslims. The president made clear that he didn't want his political agenda completely disrupted by terrorism. He pointed to education reform—No Child Left Behind—as remaining his top domestic priority.

Planning for Attack

Domestic policy . . . can only defeat us; foreign policy can kill us.
President John F. Kennedy

The president's support for the executive branch agencies in charge of national security was not just patriotic posturing. As the chief executive, he was dependent on the bureaucracy for a response to the terrorist attacks. He didn't need a public debate among the agencies degenerating into a blame-game on who was at fault. Bush first turned to the military when he was on Air Force One flying to Washington on September 11. Phoning Secretary of Defense Donald Rumsfeld, he said, "The ball will be in your court." But even in a national emergency, moving the bureaucracy to action would not prove to be a slam dunk.[8]

On a conference call later that day with the National Security Council, the CIA reported with "near certainty" that Osama bin Laden was behind the attack. At least three known operatives of al-Qaeda were on the passenger lists of the doomed airplanes. While the president wanted a strong response to the terrorists based in Afghanistan ("I don't want to put a million-dollar missile on a five dollar tent."), he would find that the military had no plans for invading that country or for dealing with bin Laden's terrorist network. The CIA, however, was ready. Its plan to overthrow the Taliban rulers of Afghanistan was already making its way to the president for approval on September 11. Now some wondered whether the bureaucracy had moved fast enough to counter this long-identified threat.

Not every policy decision was reached systematically in the initial confusing hours of the crisis. In his speech on that first night, the president made what journalist Bob Woodward called "one of the most significant foreign policy decisions in years"—the so-called Bush Doctrine. His statement—"We will make no distinction between those who planned these acts and those who harbor them"—announced a policy that could lead to conflict with any number of countries. It was a personal decision made in discussions with speechwriters by a president who trusted his own gut instincts. Bush had consulted with his National Security advisor, Condoleezza Rice, who after initial hesitation went along. Secretary of State Colin Powell, hurrying back from Peru at the time, had not been involved in the policy pronouncement.[9]

How would the response by various agencies of the executive branch be managed? Vice-President Cheney raised the issue of coordination to the president. A savvy bureaucratic in-fighter, Cheney offered to chair a war cabinet of the principals who would develop options for the president and streamline decisionmaking. Instead, Bush kept the reins of power in his own hands. He asserted that as commander-in-chief he would chair the full meetings of the National Security Council. When he was not attending, his National Security advisor, Ms. Rice, would run the meetings of principals. Bush wanted to signal that he was calling the shots. Cheney, knowing that his job was to serve the president, accepted a lesser role.

By September 15 in a weekend conference at the Camp David presidential retreat, the key decisions were made. The president approved an anti-terrorist war on many fronts—intelligence, finance, diplomacy, and military. The attorney general and the FBI were directed to preempt future strikes and to request new authority from Congress to track, wiretap, and stop terrorists—a decision confirming the USA Patriot Act already before the legislature. Bush signed a presidential intelligence order giving new broad authority for CIA covert operations against al-Qaeda, which included intelligence operatives in some eighty countries and the use of deadly force against the terrorist leadership. The president approved all of the CIA requests, rejecting Defense Department efforts to scale back the role of its rival agency. The military was permitted to use missiles, bombers, and "boots on the ground" in Afghanistan. They were prodded to negotiate base rights and speed their forces into position for an invasion. The issue of expanding the war to other countries was deferred—though not for long. On November 21, just seventy-two days after the terrorist attacks, President Bush asked Secretary of Defense Rumsfeld to secretly begin constructing a war plan for Iraq.[10]

Bush was aware of his crucial role in linking these closed-door executive decisions to his public/ceremonial activities. As quoted by Bob Woodward, the president remarked later,

> "I knew full well that if we could rally the American people behind a long and difficult chore, that our job would be easier. . . . I am a

product of the Vietnam era. I remember presidents trying to wage
wars that were very unpopular, and the nation split." He pointed to
a portrait of Abraham Lincoln that hung in the Oval Office. "He's
on the wall because the job of the president is to unite the nation.
That's the job of the president. And I felt like, that I had the job of
making sure the American people understood. They understood
the severity of the attack. But I wasn't sure if they understood how
long it was going to take and what a difficult process this would be."[11]

Congress Salutes

Many of the president's apparently symbolic activities following the attack had
a policy goal: to maintain the support of the public and the Congress for the
military plans he was drawing up with his security advisors.

As the initial confusion following the attacks faded, Congress united behind
the president, at least for a while. Congress's deference to the president in the
midst of an international crisis followed a long tradition in American history.
Wars have centralized power in the executive office and elevated presidents
like Abraham Lincoln, Woodrow Wilson, and Franklin Roosevelt. Despite its
constitutional powers to restrain a president, including funding for military
operations, Congress has rarely refused to support a war. In a fast-moving crisis, Congress knew that it lacked the information and expertise to challenge a
president, especially a modern chief executive with his access to the resources
of the executive branch. Congress was hard-wired to believe that a president
should control foreign policy in a crisis. Public opinion weighed in behind the
president, demanding a united front against foreign enemies and shunning
partisan "bickering" by Congress.[12]

Not surprisingly, then, the first congressional response reflected near unanimous support for the president. On September 14, after little debate, all but
one member of Congress voted for a Use-of-Force Resolution to give the president the authority to retaliate against those responsible for 9/11. The resolution was described by one scholar as "stunning in the breadth of authority it
granted." It allowed the president to "use all necessary and appropriate force
against those nations, organizations, or persons he determines planned, authorized, committed, or aided the terrorist attacks that occurred on September 11,
2001, or harbored such organizations or persons." It was the legal basis for
war against Afghanistan. But it could have been used against Iraq or Iran or
Saudi Arabia, if they had aided the terrorists. Essentially, Congress signed a
blank check: declaring war and then leaving it to the president to decide who
the enemy was.[13]

An unusually close working relationship between the president and congressional leaders continued in the weeks that followed. Every Tuesday or Wednesday at 7:00 a.m., the leaders of both parties in Congress met with the president for breakfast. No aides were permitted at these private meetings of what was called the "Gang of Five." Out of these unprecedented meetings came a supplemental appropriations bill to fund disaster relief and military operations. The head of the Democrats in the House, Minority Leader Richard A. Gephardt, reflected the political atmosphere and the legislature's deference to the executive: "We are working together here in the Congress in a completely nonpartisan way. There is no division between parties, between the Congress and the president."[14]

The Press and the Public Rally

It's hard to do jokes because, as you know, Bush is smart now.
Jay Leno

There also wasn't much division between the media and the executive. In its coverage of the attacks and of the president, the press became, in one scholar's words, "a patriot." In analyzing the attack, reporters soon dropped the historic analogy with Pearl Harbor, perhaps because the administration was concerned that it implied a lack of preparedness. The visual that came to represent the attack switched from the burning towers to the more inspiring photo of firefighters raising the American flag, Iwo Jima–like, at the site. The White House framed the reasons for the attacks: The terrorists hated the fundamental principles of the American system. As Bush put it, "They hate our freedoms." And in a later speech he said, "We wage a war to save civilization itself." The advantage of this frame was that it put the nation in a position of having its basic values under attack and thus forced to respond. If the alternative to "Why do they hate us?" was "Why do they hate our policies?" that might change the responses arising from the attack. This policy frame was discarded by the administration and ignored by the press.[15]

The president's personal character was improving in the public arena. The media, which had formerly been skeptical, if not cynical, about the president's intelligence, now saw few flaws. Earlier, George W. Bush's image was that of someone on the losing end of a war with the English language. The press frequently used these verbal slips as a sign of incompetence. Now the verbal fumbling was either ignored or considered unimportant. Perhaps the media's less cynical approach reflected the public's wish to see in the president the qualities they needed their leader to have. Even the late-night comics kept their hands off the president. In the months before 9/11, Bush was the target of 32 percent of the jokes on late-night television. In the two months following the attacks, he was the target of only 4 percent.[16]

Americans' rallying behind their government and president after 9/11 was attributed to instinct. But with leaders of the opposition Democrats and the mainstream press following the patriotic path of loyalty to national symbols— and the presidency was one—it would be surprising to find much vocal dissent among the general public. Americans faced an international threat they hadn't thought much about before—a 1998 poll showed that only 4 percent of the public identified terrorism as an important issue. Now demonstrations of solidarity, mixed with vengeance toward the enemy, were the immediate and near universal public response.

The president's ratings skyrocketed, from the low 50s to over 90 percent approval, an almost unprecedented rise. Even rarer was how long Bush's support remained high. Some six months later, it had only barely dropped. This support for the president was paralleled by a rise in trust for all government institutions. The thirty-year decline in trust for the federal government, rooted in the lies and tragedies of Vietnam and Watergate, was reversed temporarily by the trauma of the terrorist attacks. Strong backing for an armed response was also evident. An *ABC News/Washington Post* poll taken on the evening of September 11 showed that 90 percent advocated the use of the military against those responsible for the attacks. This aggressive nationalism extended to actions toward terrorist suspects detained in the United States without benefit of civil liberties protections. A *Newsweek* poll found that 86 percent of the public supported the government detention of accused terrorists.[17]

What had been a widespread public cynicism toward politics—reinforced by the media frenzy of the Lewinsky scandal and the nasty partisan controversies in Florida over the 2000 election—dissolved in an outpouring of patriotism. American flags were hung from highway overpasses next to signs proclaiming: *These colors don't run.* Even if these national sentiments would quiet in time, they would define the public opinion boundaries of Washington politics for months to come.

Limits of Bipartisanship

> **The Constitution is "an invitation to struggle for the privilege of directing American foreign policy."**
>
> Edward S. Corwin, *The President: Office and Powers, 1787–1957*

In the weeks following September 11, criticism of the president was limited, feeble, and angrily put down when it surfaced. Only when important, conflicting domestic interests were in play did cracks appear in the chief executive's dominance. Then Wildavsky's division between presidential strength on national security and weakness in facing domestic interests more easily applied.

On issues touching the war, where patriotic appeals didn't ensure loyalty, the president's GOP supporters were prepared to use heavier clubs. In February 2002 Senate Democratic Majority Leader Tom Daschle told reporters that he believed the war on terrorism was successful but he worried that the administration's efforts to expand the war lacked "a clear direction." One Republican House leader called the remarks "disgusting." Trent Lott, Senate Minority Leader, attacked: "How dare Senator Daschle criticize President Bush while we are fighting our war on terrorism, especially when we have troops in the field?" And Rep. Tom Davis, chairman of the National Republican Congressional Campaign Committee, accused Daschle of "giving aid and comfort to our enemies," which just happens to be the legal definition of treason. Few Democrats came to Daschle's defense.[18]

But bipartisanship had its limits. Congress was willing to quickly pass the administration's USA Patriot Act, which loosened a number of the restraints governing surveillance activities. But congressional concern for the consequences on individual privacy led it to "sunset" the most controversial provisions, meaning they would expire in 2005 unless Congress voted to renew them. As the country moved further from 9/11, Congress stiffened resistance to presidential initiatives, including drilling in the Arctic Wildlife Reserve and judicial nominations, judging that the argument that dissent on these domestic issues would hurt the war effort was strained at best.

Beneath the surface unity, Washington interest groups didn't change their goals. They reframed their arguments to speak to the new crisis. The preferred response to terrorism depended on the lobbyists making the pitch. The airline and insurance industries, which suffered huge losses from the attacks, made their case for assistance. More of a stretch was the travel industry, which wanted a $1,000 tax credit for family vacation expenses, or large corporations' request for a $15 billion retroactive tax break, or the makers of traffic signs wanting federal money so that Americans could escape from terrorist attacks easier, or the California date growers who lobbied for California dates being included in Afghan food packages. As one lobbyist admitted, "What happened was a tragedy, certainly, but there are opportunities. We're in business. This is not a charity."[19]

Bipartisan congressional cooperation with the president floundered on the issue of airport security. The fact that all the al-Qaeda hijackers had passed through security led many Americans to fear flying. Airport traffic declined, and Congress examined what it could do. The problem wasn't hard to locate. Airport security guards, some getting $7 an hour, made less than fast-food restaurant workers. Turnover was high, training was haphazard, and security breaches were frequent. For congressional Democrats, the solution was to create a new agency in the Department of Transportation where professional screeners could be hired and trained. Such legislation easily passed the Senate, 100-0.

But the majority Republicans in the House took a dim view of expanding federal employment. They wanted to continue to have private companies handling airport security, though with better standards, salaries, and training. They also worried about the difficulty in firing incompetent security personnel protected by civil service rules. Not as loudly expressed was the GOP concern that this reform meant 40,000 new federal employees, who could be expected to join a Democratic labor union, look to the Democrats to protect their interests, and donate campaign funds to Democratic candidates. Ideologically, Republicans preferred solutions resting on private corporations, which were also more likely than government workers to contribute to GOP candidates.

Public opinion made the difference. Anxiety about security was reinforced by press stories of private firms hiring convicted criminals as screeners and cutting corners on safety to save money. People felt safer having federal employees responsible for airport security. At the same time, the crash of American Airlines Flight 587 in Queens, New York, just two months after the 9/11 attacks seemed to mobilize public opinion. Although the crash had nothing to do with terrorism, the public pressure about airline safety grew. The White House and congressional Republicans caved. While some concessions were made, such as allowing federal screeners to be dismissed for incompetence, the bill that resulted was a Democratic victory over the president.[20]

A Call to Arms

The climax of the initial response to the attack came in President Bush's speech to a joint session of Congress on September 20. Using the Capitol as his stage and the Congress as his cheering chorus, a president not known for rhetoric gave an inspiring speech. He called on the nation to unite to destroy terrorism. "Tonight we are a country awakened to danger and called to defend freedom. Our grief has turned to anger, and anger to resolution. Whether we bring our enemies to justice, or bring justice to our enemies, justice will be done."

He framed the challenge as one that Americans had faced in the past. "They hate our freedoms—our freedom of religion, our freedom of speech, our freedom to vote and assemble and disagree with each other. . . . We have seen their kind before. They are the heirs of all the murderous ideologies of the twentieth century . . . They follow in the path of fascism, and Nazism and totalitarianism. And they will follow that path all the way, to where it ends: in history's unmarked grave of discarded lies."

Bush saw a long, difficult campaign to which he committed the resources of the nation. He pledged, "The advance of human freedom—the great achievement of our time, and the great hope of every time—now depends on us . . . We will not tire, we will not falter, and we will not fail." And when Bush concluded, "In our grief and anger, we have found our mission and our moment," he wasn't speaking only of the nation. He was speaking for his presidency.

In time, the national unity behind the president would fade. A short conflict in Afghanistan was followed by a far different involvement in Iraq. Misleading presidential justifications that Iraq had weapons of mass destruction and was closely allied to the al-Qaeda terrorists undermined the public support that followed 9/11. As the costs and casualties of the Iraq War mounted, the gaps in military planning became more apparent and an end to the violence grew more distant. Political leaders, the press, and the public would not rally behind the president as they had after 9/11. The doubts about presidential leadership of foreign policy took center stage in the 2004 election. Critics claimed that this was due to the administration's incompetence, lack of candor, and arrogant unwillingness to accept responsibility for mistakes. But it may also have reflected a system working the way it was designed. The period following the terrorist attacks was the exception. Even in foreign policy, presidents remain part of a government where, as James Madison stated, "Ambition must be made to counteract ambition."[21]

Notes

1. Aaron Wildavsky, "The Two Presidencies," *Trans-Action* 4, no. 2 (December 1966): 7–14. The article has been widely reprinted, and the quote can be found in Peter Woll, ed., *American Government: Readings and Cases* (New York: Longman, 1999), 306.
2. James M. Lindsay, "Deference and Defiance: The Shifting Rhythm of Executive-Legislative Relations in Foreign Policy." *Presidential Studies Quarterly* 33, no. 3 (September 2003): 537. The quote in the first paragraph is Lindsay's.
3. Frank Bruni, *Ambling into History,* 255, quoted by Kathleen Hall Jamieson and Paul Waldman, *The Press Effect* (New York: Oxford University Press, 2003), 146.
4. *USA Today,* September 12, 2001, as quoted by *National Journal,* September 15, 2001, 2856.
5. Jeremy D. Mayer, *9-11: The Giant Awakens* (Belmont, CA: Wadsworth/Thomson, 2003), 24.
6. "Emotional Bush Promises Victory," *Boston Globe,* September 14, 2001.
7. See Thomas Langston, *With Reverence and Contempt: How Americans Think About Their President* (Baltimore: Johns Hopkins University Press, 1995).
8. Bob Woodward, *Bush at War* (New York: Simon & Schuster, 2002), 19. The internal national security discussions leading to the invasion of Afghanistan are taken from the Woodward book. Woodward, an editor at the *Washington Post,* was given unique access to the participants in these meetings and granted extensive interviews that

included the president. His book can be considered the administration's version of the executive branch planning for the war in Afghanistan.

9. Woodward, 30–31.

10. Bob Woodward, *Plan of Attack* (New York: Simon & Schuster, 2004), 1. Bush's Secretary of the Treasury Paul O'Neill says that the president had brought up using force against Iraq back in January 2001. See Ron Suskind, *The Price of Loyalty* (New York: Simon & Schuster, 2004), Chapter 2.

11. Woodward, *Bush at War,* 95.

12. See Gary C. Jacobson and Samuel Kernel, *The Logic of American Politics in Wartime* (Washington, DC: Congressional Quarterly Press, 2004), 9–16.

13. Lindsay, 538.

14 *CQ Weekly,* September 15, 2001, 2124.

15. Jamieson and Waldman, Chapter 6, "The Press as Patriot."

16. Jamieson and Waldman, 157–161.

17. Mayer.

18. As quoted by Lindsay, 538.

19. David E. Rosenbaum, "Since Sept. 11, Lobbyists Use New Pitches for Old Pleas," New York Times on the Web, *www.nytimes.com,* December 3, 2001.

20. Lindsay.

21. The phrase is from James Madison, *The Federalist* #51.

chapter 12

The *Columbia* and *Challenger* Disasters

Groupthink in a Bureaucracy

Modern government needs bureaucracy. To deliver the mail, to fight the wars, to clean the environment, to manage the schools, and to launch shuttles into space, an organization of experts and staff is required. These administrators are what keep America's government among the most competent, least corrupt in the world. But there's a price to be paid for relying on specialized bureaucracies. The risk is they can develop interests of their own, often seeing the world through the eyes of their agency's mission rather than the citizens they serve. They may also be so tightly directed or politically pressured that they ignore the expertise on which their organization depends.

The National Aeronautics and Space Administration (NASA) is a highly regarded federal agency, with accomplishments in space exploration that include putting men on the moon and robots on Mars. Yet our case study, somewhat unfairly, focuses on the agency's two most spectacular disasters—the *Columbia* and *Challenger* shuttle accidents. Both occurred because of flawed technology—foam insulation hitting the *Columbia* on takeoff, and O-rings eroding on the *Challenger* rocket boosters. Both problems surfaced as risks before the tragedies occurred. But bureaucratic pressures led to both flaws being minimized, the people raising them ignored. The immediate causes of the accidents were technical; the underlying reasons were organizational.

The accidents occurred seventeen years apart, the *Columbia* in 2003, the *Challenger* in 1986, yet the bureaucratic behavior was similar. At the risk of simplifying complex technical and bureaucratic issues, one shared problem was "groupthink," the striving for in-group agreement that overrides a realistic appraisal of alternatives by discouraging independent thinking.[1] While groupthink can promote a loyal, smoothly running team, in this case a downsized organization accountable to high external expectations pressured employees not to break ranks.

Thanks to Professor Melvin J. Dubnick for his comments on an earlier draft of this chapter.

Engineering experts' advice was undermined by supervisors needing to keep costs down, to meet a demanding schedule, to retain a vital contract, to emphasize a "can-do" attitude, and to hold on to the bureaucratic procedures that had served them in the past. NASA's very virtues were its vices. A hardworking bureaucracy's dedication to its mission encouraged a culture of consensus that reduced internal conflict, but produced the mistakes leading to both tragedies.

---

concepts highlighted

1. Bureaucrats are often represented as unmotivated administrators. This case reveals people dedicated to their **bureaucracy's goals** and committed to maximizing limited resources. How did high motivation lead to errors in implementation? How was NASA cutting corners and ignoring safety to achieve its mission?

2. **Downsizing** the federal government by reducing bureaucracy's employees and budgets is politically popular. This case study shows some of its internal consequences. How did it affect NASA? Since the agency didn't want to give up its shuttle missions, how did it try to achieve ambitious goals with fewer resources? Did privatization—contracting out to private contractors like Morton Thiokol—change how NASA bureaucrats did their jobs?

3. All bureaucracies are structured as hierarchies, with bosses and subordinates, usually divided into specialized areas of expertise. How did this **bureaucratic structure** encourage groupthink and discourage open discussions? How did NASA leadership limit information and control the decisions that the agency made?

4. Making bureaucracies **politically accountable** to elected officials is important. But did NASA's leadership's accountability create the pressures that made the groupthink behind the accidents more acceptable? How did congressional oversight, politically influenced contracts, and public relations concerns affect NASA's operations?

The *Columbia* Crash, February 1, 2003[2]

Just sixteen minutes before its scheduled landing at the Kennedy Space Center in Florida, the space shuttle *Columbia* disintegrated during reentry. On that morning of February 1, 2003, flashes of the orbiter debris could be seen across the skies from California to Texas. Even as Mission Control at Kennedy was attempting to contact the *Columbia,* people outside called to say they had seen live television coverage of the spacecraft breaking up. It was a catastrophic accident that cost the lives of the seven-person crew, the first shuttle disaster since *Challenger* crashed on January 28, 1986.

Earlier, as those on duty at Mission Control tracked the *Columbia* descending at eight times faster than a bullet, the first sign of trouble was the failure of four sensors on the left wing. The entry flight director's thoughts flashed back to the launch: A briefcase-sized piece of foam insulation had broken off from *Columbia*'s external fuel tank eighty-one seconds after liftoff and slammed into the left wing. A team of experts had studied photos of foam flying off and dismissed its importance. The Mission Management Team had unanimously agreed. This failure in the left wing had to be a coincidence.[3]

But seven months later the head of NASA's Research Center would declare, "In four simple words, the foam did it."[4] The foam, traveling 500 miles per hour, had punched a hole as big as a dinner plate in the ceramic edge of the left wing. It was invisible to the astronauts in orbit. As the shuttle reentered the atmosphere, heat passed through the hole and melted out the inside of the wing. Foam had caused the accident, but a cluster of bureaucratic attitudes had led to the disaster.

Two sets of decisions and non-decisions led to the events in the sky on that morning in February. The first was what happened in the months and years before the launch that led to a NASA mindset that foam was "no big deal." The second was what occurred once the foam had struck and the shuttle was in orbit. Here a series of decisions about what to do, specifically whether to get military spy satellites to take a picture of any damage, sealed *Columbia*'s fate. In both arenas, an organizational culture—call it groupthink or "group pride"—led to a disaster that eerily paralleled the *Challenger* disaster seventeen years earlier.

Columbia: Foam Oversight

> *. . . For twenty years NASA management had lived under the belief that foam could cause no damage.*
>
> Dr. Douglas Osheroff, Nobel laureate and member of the
> Columbia Accident Investigation Board

In every one of the 112 shuttle missions before *Columbia*'s January 2003 liftoff, foam had hit the shuttle, including some severe strikes. On *Columbia*'s first shuttle flight in 1981, 300 protective heat tiles had been dinged by a shower of foam. During the twenty-one years since, orbiters had returned with an average of 143 damaged tiles, including thirty-one with scars measuring more than an inch. The foam, used to insulate the external tanks, had been deemed an "accepted risk" despite a clear rule against debris strikes that had existed from the beginning of the shuttle program. No substitute was found for the foam (which looked and felt like its cousin, Styrofoam), and efforts to reduce its thickness had not solved the problem. The more it fell off and struck the craft

Saddened NASA employees absorb the news of the *Columbia* shuttle's fatal reentry early in 2003.
Bill Ingalls/NASA/AP–Wide World Photos

without causing an accident, the more the bureaucrats agreed among themselves: Foam was a nuisance, not a "safety-of-flight" issue.[5]

This view was put to the test at the launch of the shuttle *Atlantis* in October 2002, when a mailbox-size chunk of foam struck the rocket booster. Both the size of the debris and the fact that it had hit near a critical electronics box had caused jaws to drop when film of it was shown at the Flight Center. Working-level engineers wanted the foam loss to be declared an IFA—In-Flight-Anomaly—a critical failure that had to be fixed before the next flight or proved not to threaten vehicle safety. Engineers saw the largest piece of debris to come off the space vehicle as a dangerous threat. Yet the argument they faced from their bosses was that the size of this debris was unique, that it did no damage, and that there was no available alternative. Instead of being classified as IFA, it was put under a milder "Plans/Studies." Responding to pressures to keep to the schedule, supervisors stifled dissent. One engineer who resisted this group pressure and to signing the flight readiness statement for the next shuttle was privately given a brief history of foam loss, how it had been handled in the past, and how it had never interfered with a launch before. After listening to his superior, he signed.

Senior managers discussed the foam issue, along with other concerns, at the Flight Readiness Review for the shuttle *Endeavor*'s November flight. The fuel tank manager who presented the foam issue to the meeting had not been impressed by the strike on the *Atlantis*, equating it to a Styrofoam cooler lid hitting the window of a car—distracting but not dangerous. In his seven-minute presentation, he dismissed safety concerns as no more relevant than they had been for all the previous flights. He promised to report back on possible fixes for the foam problem. The meeting participants took no formal action and set the due date for a report on the issue for after the next shuttle launch. Essentially, the problem was buried.

The *Endeavor* was launched on November 23. As the fuel tank manager had predicted, the shuttle suffered no serious foam damage. The issue never came up at the next Flight Readiness Review for the *Columbia*. A senior NASA manager, looking back at the *Endeavor*'s Readiness Review, would later conclude, "That was one of the things we really missed as an agency."[6]

External pressures played a role in the decision to continue with the *Columbia* launch as planned. NASA was in the midst of a large downsizing, with its shuttle workforce having dropped 42 percent in the decade before the *Columbia* launch—from 30,000 to just over 17,000. It had been reducing its budget and employment by eliminating civil service jobs and increasing the use of outside private contractors. Despite the downsizing, NASA was still over-budget and behind schedule in assembling the Space Station, which was the primary task of the shuttles. If it didn't meet its goal of assembling crucial parts of the Space Station by early 2004, it risked losing support from the White House and Congress. NASA was not just politically accountable; it was "on probation." The Columbia Accident Investigation Board (CAIB) later reported that the managers' need to keep to their schedule "appeared to have influenced their decision" not to treat the foam loss as an IFA. NASA was "slowly accepting additional risk in trying to meet a schedule that probably could not be met."[7]

Columbia: **Following the Launch**

The story that emerged was a sad and unnecessary one, involving arrogance, insularity, and bad luck allowed to run unchecked.

William Langewiesche, *Atlantic Monthly*

Shouts of "Oh my God!" filled the film lab. Launch engineers were watching film of a large chunk of foam smashing into the *Columbia*'s left wing at the shuttle's takeoff a few hours before. It had come from the same area of the fuel tank as the one that had broken off in October. But this debris was by far the largest piece to hit the orbiter. It wasn't clear from the pictures exactly where it had struck or whether the debris cloud contained foam, ice, or bits of the shuttle's heat tiles. It *was* clear that this time it wasn't the rocket booster that was hit. It was the orbiter itself.

The film reviewers concluded that the vehicle might have suffered damage from this unprecedented strike, but that they couldn't tell conclusively from these pictures. They suggested getting the military to use their spy satellites to take pictures of the shuttle in orbit. Rumors soon spread at Kennedy that the shuttle might be landing early. Some managers put out reassuring e-mails downplaying the likely damage from the foam and emphasizing the strength of the heat tiles in the wing edge area.

The Mission managers responded to the film with minimal concern and a desire to get on with the mission. Worried engineers on the working-level Debris Assessment Team found that they had to clearly prove that a safety issue existed before the Shuttle management would request a spy-satellite image of the left wing. (As the CAIB later noted, proving something is *unsafe* reversed the usual requirement to prove that a situation *is safe.*) Senior managers pointed out the extra time that would be spent maneuvering the *Columbia* into position for the pictures, the halting of scientific experiments, and the uncertainty whether the new images would be very clear. They doubted that the foam had sufficient density to damage the spacecraft. Managers also made the fatalistic argument that even if there was damage, it couldn't be repaired in orbit. The NASA supervisors, under budgetary and political pressures, were interested in how to keep the foam problem from affecting the schedules of future shuttles, not in generating information undermining their decisions.

Some frustrated engineers used a computer program called Crater, which could predict damage from debris fragments on a spacecraft. From the large foam chunk's size, direction, and impact site, the model calculated that the strike would have disastrously penetrated the heat tiles. But senior managers dismissed the Crater model as not appropriate for large debris. They assumed that the foam had hit heat tiles—not the wing edge—and couldn't have damaged them. Other engineers requested, through informal channels, Air Force photos of the left wing. When the chair of the Mission Management Team found out, she simply terminated the request with the Department of Defense. The photos were never taken.[8]

According to the CAIB report, the organizational culture of NASA deterred working-level engineers from vigorously pushing their safety concerns. Rodney Rocha, described as a smart, stubborn, veteran NASA engineer, was upset by the foam strike. He had pushed for satellite photos and argued with others about the likelihood of shuttle damage. At a pre–Mission Management Team meeting where the foam strike was discussed, Rocha and other engineers felt that the dangers were minimized and the meeting rushed. Yet Rocha sat and said nothing. It was a large meeting with a consensus among the supervisors that there was no safety-of-flight issue. Although they talked about heat tile problems, no mention was made of possible damage to the wing edge panels. Reflecting on his resentment at this groupthink, Rocha recalled his feelings as the meeting ended: "I felt like going in there and interrupting or waiting until they got through and just saying, . . . I just want you to know that we are not finished,' but I didn't. I didn't do any such thing. . . ."[9]

An atmosphere of intimidation prevailed, and with it came an unspoken fear of reprisals for criticism. The Debris Assessment Team's concerns never made it up to the Mission Management Team supervising the shuttle. Senior managers never asked the engineers about their concerns. The safety representatives were too few and too passive. No one challenged the shuttle managers' decisions, including the assumption that rescuing the *Columbia* was impossible. Later, the head of the CAIB concluded that launching a second shuttle in time to attempt a rescue would not have been easy but was conceivable. Indeed, it was the rescue of the *Apollo 13* crew in 1970 from its seemingly certain disaster in space that had given the agency much of its heroic public image. A NASA astronaut said, "You give us a challenge, we know the problem, and it is amazing what you can do."[10]

But in the *Columbia* tragedy NASA's directors first had to agree that they faced a problem. They didn't. Even worse, it had all happened before.

Challenger: January 28, 1986

I think I'm hearing an echo here.

Sally Ride, former astronaut and member of the two commissions
that investigated both the *Columbia* and *Challenger* disasters

Seventeen years earlier, the space shuttle Challenger *had been postponed four times before it took off in 1986 on its tenth mission. A little over a minute into the flight, a massive explosion destroyed the spacecraft, killing the crew of seven. It was the space program's worst disaster yet and a remembered tragedy for the millions who watched on TV. The commission created to investigate the explosion found design flaws in the O-rings of the Solid Rocket Boosters, but also identified NASA's faulty decisionmaking system as a cause of the accident. A look back at a key meeting the night before the launch illuminates how "rooted in history" this accident was, and how critical group decisions would lead to the first shuttle disaster.*

On the night of January 27, 1986, thirty-four people sat at tables in three different states and held a tense two-hour teleconference. They were managers and engineers from NASA's Kennedy Space Center in Florida, the Marshall

Space Flight Center in Alabama, and, in Utah, representatives from Morton Thiokol, the private contractor who had built the Solid Rocket Boosters to be used in the next day's launch of the *Challenger*. Several meetings had already taken place on whether it was safe to launch the shuttle, and the debate centered around whether the O-rings that sealed the joints of the boosters would hold.

The engineers from Morton Thiokol, led by Roger Boisjoly, presented their doubts about the O-rings. The Booster contained two levels of seals, a primary and a secondary seal. Both seals were designed to be resilient enough on take-off to expand and close up the joints. If the primary O-ring did not seal, hot gas could be blown through to the secondary O-ring, possibly causing it to fail and resulting in a catastrophe. Boisjoly and the engineers had seen some evidence from previous flights that when the temperature at launch was cold, the O-rings lost their ability to seal. Because the weather at the launch the next morning was predicted to be an unusually chilly 18 degrees, the Thiokol engineers recommended against launching.

Thiokol engineers had never before recommended against a launch. Boisjoly's team of engineers had been studying the O-ring problem for several months, without much support from management. Although the evidence was mixed, their engineering hunches and safety concerns had led to the prelaunch meeting. The teleconference the night before the launch was in itself unusual, since such presentations were usually made face-to-face two weeks before a launch. And the predicted cold temperature was below that of any previous launch. NASA was venturing into uncharted territory.[11]

As in the *Columbia* disaster almost two decades later, both internal and external pressures were pushing for the launch. Everyone at the meeting was familiar with NASA's mission-oriented, low-cost bureaucratic culture. This meant that whatever priority was given to safety in speeches had to compete with concerns of schedule and expense in practice. Where once the burden of proof was on engineers to show beyond a doubt that it was safe to launch, now Morton Thiokol was expected to prove that launching *Challenger* would *not* be safe. If NASA accepted the engineers' recommendation not to launch below 53 degrees (the previous lowest temperature of a launch), the managers would be agreeing to a new criterion for all launches—a costly complication in meeting tight schedules for future missions.

An underlying conflict existed in the bureaucratic hierarchy between managers and engineers. Earlier in NASA's history, the professional opinions of technical people—scientists and engineers, no matter what their rank—were given great deference. Over the years, a more top-down system of bureaucratic accountability had developed. Managers and engineers fell into a relationship of superior and subordinate. The experts began to act like "cowed bureaucrats," and the free flow of information up and down the agency was restricted.[12]

The last launching of the *Challenger* shuttle in 1986. Note the two white booster rockets attached to the sides of the dark fuel tank.
Bruce Weaver/AP–Wide World Photos

Anything that "slowed" the progress of space flights, which in this case included safety concerns, was discouraged. The managers challenged the engineers' observations from previous flights, questioning whether they could be considered "hard data." Near the end of the January 27 meeting, a supervisor asked one of the engineers, "Am I the only one who wants to fly?" and requested one of them to "take off his engineering hat and put on his management hat."[13]

While NASA officials at the teleconference disagreed that low temperature led to O-ring erosion, they were reluctant to overrule the engineers at the meeting. At this point Thiokol managers asked for a smaller private caucus with their engineers. Here the lead person said that "a management decision was necessary." The four senior executives then held a brief discussion and voted unanimously to reverse the original engineering recommendation. They returned to the teleconference, from which the engineers were now excluded, and announced that Thiokol had reexamined the data and supported the decision to launch. The launch managers at Marshall and Kennedy did not know that the Thiokol engineers still objected. One manager at Marshall asked, "Does anybody have anything more to say?" No one spoke. The disastrous launch went ahead the next morning.

Challenging Management

The Thiokol engineers were battling the weight of management in trying to stop the launch because of their concern for the O-rings. They were subordinates in a bureaucratic hierarchy; and their objections were dismissed as observational and intuitive, rather than quantitative and scientific. A cost-conscious culture and an array of political and economic pressures all pushed for the overriding goal of the organization—launching the shuttle. Not surprisingly then, their immediate supervisors never communicated the engineers' objections to superiors at NASA because these supervisors viewed this decision as one appropriately made at their level. Reflecting the flawed communication flows in the agency, they kept the information to themselves.[14]

Rejecting the engineers' concerns came in part from the managers' awareness that concerns with the O-rings, as well as other risk factors in the boosters, had been raised in prior launches. As the missions continued and the O-rings showed damage but didn't fail, the range of "acceptable risks" expanded. NASA may have been "playing Russian roulette," as a member of the Rogers Commission later concluded, but each decision accepting a higher level of risk made the next decision that much easier. Soon it became routine, what one scholar called the "normalization of deviance." Step by step, the shuttle management descended into poor judgment.[15]

Financial and political pressures were another fact of life for those overseeing the shuttles. Budgets were tight. The public climate that NASA operated in was not as supportive of the shuttle program as it had been during the "space race" to the moon in the 1960s. For the *Apollo*'s journey to the moon, Congress had just about written NASA a blank check, with little accountability to the rest of the government. But now the shuttle program had to be sold as a business, with NASA claiming it could pay its own way by ferrying scientific experiments and commercial satellites to space and back. As a result, the shuttle was publicly positioned as a routine "operational program" rather than the more risky "developmental system." The four reusable shuttles were put on an ambitious schedule of seventeen missions a year with twenty-four scheduled for 1988.

This meant speeding up the turnaround time of shuttles between launches, and making sure the 60 million components and thousands of count-down activities would not interfere with takeoff.

As the demands increased and the resources tightened, the need for political support steered NASA away from the technical culture on which the space agency had built its reputation for quality. Contracts were let out to a variety of contractors for most shuttle activities, which meant that the original "dirty hands" approach of NASA technicians doing the work themselves changed into the supervising of contractors. Nor were these contracts devoid of political calculations. One agency critic said, "NASA was organized from day one so that all fifty states would have NASA contracts. . . ."[16] Politics might mean placing a U.S. senator in orbit, or choosing a New Hampshire woman to be the "First Teacher in Space" for public relations purposes. (That teacher, Christa McAuliffe, was lost with the other six crew members aboard the *Challenger.*)

The private companies' managers were aware of these pressures surrounding the shuttle program. As contractors they could be expected to respond to their bureaucratic employers, not just to the engineers whom they employed. Privatization of the space program had led to Thiokol's $1 billion contract with NASA, which was up for renegotiation with a serious possibility that it would be put up for bidding to competitors. A phone call was scheduled for the day after the *Challenger* liftoff to discuss the contract. All the managers knew this. One can only imagine the impact on Thiokol when one NASA official said during the heated teleconference, "My God, Thiokol, when do you want me to launch, next April?" Immediately following this comment, the Thiokol executives asked for the private caucus with their engineers.[17]

Conclusion

Diane Vaughan, a Boston College professor and expert on bureaucracy, wrote an exhaustive and penetrating scholarly study of the 1986 *Challenger* disaster and NASA's organizational culture. Her widely reviewed book was used to improve safety programs, and she consulted on reducing risks for organizations ranging from the U.S. Forest Service to hospitals. Eventually, she was called to testify before the Columbia Accident Investigation Board at a public hearing. She was asked if NASA ever contacted her after the book came out. She replied, "No. . . . Everybody called. My high school boyfriend called. But NASA never called."[18]

Whatever the NASA bureaucracy learned from the first disaster resulted in only limited changes, too few to prevent the second accident. Investigators of the *Columbia* noted the similarities with the earlier crash: cost and schedule pressures, the increasing acceptance of risk, the top-down communications, and the ignoring of engineers' concerns. In the words of one CAIB commissioner, ". . . They basically relaxed back to the kind of thinking that they'd had that had produced the loss of the *Challenger*." NASA's dedication to accomplishing its goals led to ignoring safety. Once again groupthink was used to throttle dissent. Rather than break rank or speak against the consensus, the engineers involved in *Columbia* would give up or convince themselves that everything was OK. When someone differed from the party line "they were intimidated or ridiculed," which were, the investigators noted, "not very positive management techniques."[19]

While organizational dysfunctions became the focus for both investigations into the shuttle disasters, this should not obscure the issue of individual responsibility. "NASA" didn't approve the shuttle launches, the "Agency" didn't intimidate engineers, and the "bureaucracy" didn't overlook safety. Individuals did. People in authority responded to pressures, evaluated information, and made decisions. They also made mistakes for which they were accountable. Nor is NASA the only institution in which groupthink exists. A Senate report in the summer of 2004 showed that the CIA's exaggeration of Iraqi weapons of mass destruction served the political purpose of supporting elected officials' policy of going to war. The Senate panel blamed "a broken corporate culture and poor management."[20] But here, too, blaming systems and communications and bureaucracy, rather than individuals, may lead those responsible to evade responsibility.

Postscript

After the *Challenger* crash, Roger Boisjoly, one of Morton Thiokol's dissenting engineers, was called before the Rogers Commission. He testified that he disagreed with his managers in their interpretation of the events leading to the launch decision. Thiokol management subsequently removed him from their investigation team and criticized him for "airing the company's dirty laundry." He was isolated from NASA and their efforts to redesign the O-rings. Chairman Rogers publicly criticized Thiokol for retaliating against those who opposed the decision to launch. In an effort to clear the air, Boisjoly asked for a private meeting with the company's three top executives. He found them unreceptive. He saw his position as untenable.

On July 21, 1986, less than six months after the *Challenger* blew up, Boisjoly requested an extended sick leave from Morton Thiokol and eventually resigned. Reflecting on his experience later, he wrote, "I have been asked by some if I would testify again if I knew in advance of the potential consequences to me and my career. My answer is always an immediate 'yes.' I couldn't live with any self-respect if I tailored my actions based upon the personal consequences. . . ."[21]

Notes

1. Paul 't Hart, and Marceline Kroon, "Groupthink in Government: Pathologies of Small-Group Decision Making," in J. L. Garnett and A. Kouzmin, eds., *Handbook of Administrative Communication* (New York: Marcel Dekker, 1997), 309–328.

2. Following both the *Challenger* and *Columbia* disasters, independent investigating commissions were set up: the Rogers Commission (named for its chairman, William Rogers, former Secretary of State) following *Challenger*, and the Columbia Accident Investigation Board, CAIB (chaired by Retired Admiral Harold Gehman), after *Columbia*. The investigators produced volumes of reports that provided the basis for the writings by scholars and reporters, and much of what follows in this chapter. The conclusions of the two commissions were similar in placing blame on bureaucratic mismanagement and the striving for group consensus under the pressures of costs and schedule.

3. Michael Cabbage and William Harwood, *Comm Check . . . The Final Flight of Shuttle Columbia* (New York: Free Press, 2004), Chapter 5.

4. From "Talk of the Nation," National Public Radio, August 26, 2003.

5. Cabbage and Harwood, 56–59.

6. Cabbage and Harwood, 66–72.

7. Maureen Hogan Casamayou, "The *Columbia* Accident," in Richard J. Stillman II, *Public Administration: Concepts and Cases,* 8th ed. (Boston: Houghton Mifflin, 2005), 117. Also Cabbage and Harwood, 206.

8. From Cabbage and Harwood, Chapters 5 and 6.

9. As quoted by Cabbage and Harwood, 257, 258.

10. See William Langewiesche, "*Columbia*'s Last Flight," *Atlantic Monthly,* November 2003, 85.

11. Diane Vaughan, "The Trickle-Down Effect: Policy Decisions, Risky Work, and the *Challenger* Tragedy," *California Management Review* (Winter 1997): 92–95.

12. From B. S. Romzek and M. J. Dubnick, "Accountability in the Public Sector: Lessons from the *Challenger* Tragedy," *Public Administration Review* 47 (1987).

13. Russell P. Boisjoly, Ellen Foster Curtis, and Eugene Mellican, "Roger Boisjoly and the *Challenger* Disaster: The Ethical Dimensions," *Journal of Business Ethics* 8 (1989): 217–230.

14. Boisjoly et al., 224.

15. Vaughan.

16. Greg Klerkx, *Lost in Space: The Fall of NASA and the Dream of a New Space Age* (New York: Pantheon, 2004), 254.

17. Michael T. Charles, "The Last Flight of Space Shuttle *Challenger*," in Richard J. Stillman, *Public Administration: Concepts and Cases,* 8th ed. (Boston: Houghton Mifflin, 2005), 118–119.

18. Cabbage and Harwood, 203.

19. Cabbage and Harwood, 201.

20. *Washington Post,* July 10, 2004.

21. Boisjoly et al., 229.

chapter 13

Watergate, *U.S. v. Nixon,* and the U.S. Supreme Court

The justices of the Supreme Court sit atop one of the three branches of the federal government. They head an important policymaking institution. The Supreme Court acts as an agent of the national government in interpreting, applying, and creating rules for the country that, as seen in other cases, can range from abortion to affirmative action. At times the Court resolves disputes between groups, or even between the other branches of government. In its rulings, the Court may act to secure its own powers and the respect owed to the judicial branch. By interpreting and enforcing the law in this case, these nine policymakers became referees for the political system they help govern.

In *United States v. Nixon,* the Supreme Court confronted the national crisis called "Watergate." The 1972 wiretapping of Democratic party headquarters by agents of President Richard Nixon, and the cover-up, scandal, and resignations that followed, mark the beginning of modern American politics. Many of the themes that now occupy contemporary students flowered here. The ascendancy and danger of secretive executive power; the bitter partisan conflicts inflamed by a festering war; the rise of a cynical, adversarial media; the struggle for party and campaign reform; the acceptance of scandals and investigations as a route of opposition (marked by a *–gate* being affixed at the end of the latest Washington embarrassment); and the public's declining confidence in their government and refusal to politically participate: All these bloomed in Watergate.

Watergate began in the Nixon White House's near obsession over confidential information being leaked to newspapers by dissenters, most spectacularly in the *Pentagon Papers,* a secret government study of the decisions leading to the Vietnam War. After going to court proved unsuccessful in stopping publication, the Nixon administration tried to prosecute those responsible and then to halt other leaks by using undercover espionage agents. The same undercover agents would later plant wiretaps on the Democrats for purely partisan motives—the president's reelection. The exposure of these illegal activities poisoned the political atmosphere, isolated the president, disgusted and disillusioned the public, and led to Nixon's unprecedented resignation.

By the time the scandal reached the Supreme Court in the case of *U.S. v. Nixon,* Congress was closing in on the president's illegal activities. No reconciliation was possible between the branches. The constitutional issue centered on whether Nixon could use the doctrine of "executive privilege" to withhold taped conversations that might prove his wrongdoing. The president claimed that the judiciary had no right to judge him. Questioning the power of judicial review turned the case into an institutional challenge of the Court, one demanding a unified response from the nine "politicians" who saw their branch's authority at stake.

concepts highlighted

1. The constitutional principle of **separation of powers** was evident throughout Watergate. After the president violated the law to undermine legitimate opposition, other branches of government moved to check this expanding executive power. Note that a district judge first exposed the cover-up, Congress moved to investigate (after stories by the press were leaked by the bureaucracy), and ultimately the Supreme Court entered the dispute. Was it important that this expansion of executive power occurred in wartime? How was the Constitution's separation of powers reinforced by partisan politics?

2. The Supreme Court has been called a **political institution**, with its own policy preferences and goals. From the partisan nature of their appointments to their final decision supporting their institution and resolving the dispute, the justices acted in the political arena. What aspects of the Watergate case illustrate the Court's political role?

3. The case opens a window to the Court's internal **judicial decisionmaking**. Why did this decision unite the Court? From speeding up the case, to the conferences in the opinion writing, to the unanimous decision, the Court anticipated the reaction of the public and the other branches. Did the crisis atmosphere make the Court more sensitive to public opinion?

4. The Court not only resolved a heated conflict between the two elected branches of government, it also made law. This **judicial lawmaking** allowed for a wider interpretation of the president's claim of **executive privilege**. How did this debatable legal precedent allow for a compromise unanimous opinion?

5. **Judicial review** as applied in this case allowed an appointed branch to check an elected branch in the name of the Constitution. How did the president's questioning of judicial review affect the Court? Were the constitutional claims by the president undermined by their serving to cover up criminal behavior?

A "Third-Rate Burglary"

In the early morning hours of June 17, 1972, five men were caught breaking into the luxury Watergate building in Washington DC. They were repairing the bugging devices they had placed the month before in the offices of the Democratic National Committee. President Richard Nixon was running for re-election and the "plumbers," as the burglars were called, were illegally spying on the opposition. Two supervisors, overseeing the operation from across the street, were also arrested: E. Howard Hunt, a White House consultant and former CIA agent, and G. Gordon Liddy, employed by the Committee to Re-Elect the President (CREEP). The burglars had White House telephone numbers in their pockets.

The cover-up of White House and CREEP ties to the crime began within hours of the arrests. The problem facing the Nixon White House was that among those involved in the break-in were the president's closest aides, the directors of his campaign, the attorney general, and several high administration officials. Although the president wasn't involved in planning the break-in, he found out about its ties to his reelection within six days of the arrests. The conspiracy he led sought to prevent the exposure of this and other illegal activities, including wiretaps on reporters, the use of tax information by the IRS to target an "Enemies List," the development of a "Huston Plan" for domestic political spying, and the break-in at a psychiatrist's office to steal embarrassing files on Daniel Ellsberg, who had leaked the *Pentagon Papers* to the *New York Times*. Revealing these crimes would have jailed the president's men and dealt a major blow to his reelection.[1]

The goal of the cover-up was to make it appear that Watergate was limited to the people originally arrested. Documents linking the Oval Office to the crime were destroyed. A cover story was circulated that painted Liddy as a "wild man" who had pulled off Watergate on his own. A stickier problem was that the money used by the plumbers could be traced to the president's election campaign. Presidential aides brought the CIA in to delay the investigation by telling the FBI that tracking the money would endanger an operation. Getting the CIA to interfere with the FBI in the name of national security required Nixon's approval. Discussed within a week of the break-in, the president's involvement, when revealed on tape, would prove key to his downfall.

The cover-up continued through the November election and beyond. It succeeded in keeping Watergate away from the president's landslide victory over Democratic Senator George McGovern. Lies to the public were a constant. The president's press secretary called it a "third-rate burglary." At a press conference in August 1972, the president announced that his White House counsel had completed an investigation and that no one in the administration was involved in this "very bizarre incident." (Meanwhile, he privately congratulated White House counsel John Dean on managing a successful cover-up.) On September 15 the seven men arrested were indicted for the break-in. But the U.S. Attorneys, taking their cues from the Justice Department, treated the case as minor. No questions were asked as to why the men had committed the crime, on whose orders, and who paid them. The U.S. Attorney General called the investigation the most thorough in years, adding that there was absolutely no evidence that others should be charged.[2]

Avoiding exposure led the conspirators to commit further crimes. Campaign officials perjured themselves in trying to conceal the money going to the burglars. The head of the FBI destroyed material found in Hunt's White House safe. The president's lawyer sat in on FBI interviews of campaign officials and White House staff and reported back to his superiors. The burglars were secretly given hush money after their arrests and promised executive clemency if they remained silent. Their silence kept the lid on the scandal and the cover-up through the election on November 7, and into 1973.[3]

The Cover-up Unravels

> *President: How much money do you need?*
> *Dean: I would say these people are going to cost, uh, a million dollars*
>   *over the next, uh, two years.*
> *President: We could get that.*
>   March 21, 1973, meeting from the tapes[4]

The cover-up came apart in 1973 under persistent battering from the judiciary, the Congress, and the press. The pressure—mainly from the other branches of government guarded by the Constitution's separation of powers—turned the conspirators against each other, increased their demands for money and protection, and led to a breakdown in their silence.

While no higher-ups had been named in the trial of the burglars, presiding Judge John Sirica was not convinced that the guilty verdicts reached by the end of January had revealed the whole truth of the crime. Sirica's skepticism was backed by his power (and his reputation—he was known as "Maximum John") to impose sentences of up to sixty years in prison on the convicted plumbers. Press reports added to the climate of suspicion surrounding Watergate. Two young *Washington Post* reporters, Carl Bernstein and Bob Woodward, had been assigned the story at the time of the break-in. Their investigation of the plumbers' links to the White House convinced a wide audience that this was no ordinary robbery. Woodward and Bernstein kept Watergate on the front page and expanded the coverage to widespread "dirty tricks" against Democratic candidates. Their stories soon began to include names from Nixon's inner circle.[5]

On February 7, 1973, the Senate voted 77–0 to establish a Select Committee on Presidential Campaign Activities (under North Carolina Democratic senator Sam Ervin) to investigate Watergate and related campaign activities. Worried about their upcoming sentencing, some of the plumbers were raising their demands for hush money while threatening to reveal other illegal acts done for the White House—in short, blackmail. The Ervin Committee "invited" the president's lawyer, John Dean, to testify. The president, fearing that Watergate would blow wide open, cited "executive privilege" in refusing to allow his counsel or other aides to testify. Realizing that the cover-up was coming apart, Dean warned Nixon that Watergate had become "a cancer growing on the Presidency."[6]

Dean noticed that each of the conspirators around him was hiring a lawyer to "watch his own back." Soon one of the plumbers, facing the possibility of a lengthy jail sentence, wrote Judge Sirica that he was willing to cooperate. Within the White House, the president's closest aides were tightening the defenses around their chief. They were preparing to blame subordinates for the break-in and for keeping the president in the dark about the cover-up. Dean worried that he was being set up as the fall guy. He contacted a lawyer, and by early April he too was cooperating with prosecutors.

The Other Branches Check and Balance

> *I don't give a s _ _ _ what happens. I want you all to stonewall it. Let them plead the Fifth Amendment, cover up, or anything else that will save the plan. That's the whole point.*
>
> Richard M. Nixon, March 22, 1973, from the tapes

As the Ervin Committee began to take public testimony in televised hearings, the president responded that all members of his staff would appear voluntarily before the committee. He appeared to be cleaning house and putting the scandal behind him, dismissing his chief advisors including Attorney General John Mitchell, John Dean, and his two closest aides, H. R. (Bob) Haldeman and John Ehrlichman. Dean soon became a star witness at the committee hearings, accusing the president of involvement in both the break-in and the cover-up. Responding to a Senate resolution, Nixon's new attorney general, Elliot Richardson, appointed a special prosecutor on May 18, 1973, to investigate Watergate. This special prosecutor, Harvard professor Archibald Cox, while technically in the Justice Department, was given virtual independence from the administration. By the end of the month, Nixon publicly admitted a White House cover-up, blamed his dismissed aides, and claimed he had no prior knowledge of Watergate or the effort at concealment.

On July 16, 1973, the scandal took an unexpected turn. A former White House aide, Alexander Butterfield, when asked if there were listening devices in the Oval Office, testified that the president had taped and saved all conversations in his offices. Both Cox and the Ervin Committee immediately requested the tapes. Nixon refused. Asserting executive privilege, he maintained that the Constitution's separation of powers allowed him to withhold such confidential information from the other branches of government. The special prosecutor went into federal court to force the president to turn over nine of the tapes. Cox argued that even a president couldn't interfere with a criminal justice action in a federal court. Nixon's lawyer claimed that the president was the "sole judge of executive privilege" and that the only remedy for presidential abuse was impeachment. The president lost his case in the district court (under Judge Sirica) and then in the U.S. Court of Appeals.[7]

After a futile attempt to reach a compromise with Cox to turn over the tapes, Nixon fired the special prosecutor on October 20, 1973. This became known as the "Saturday Night Massacre," when both the attorney general and his deputy resigned rather than carry out the president's order, which they considered illegal. Facing a firestorm of national protest, the president retreated. He turned over the tapes to Judge Sirica and appointed a new special prosecutor, Leon Jaworski, who could only be fired with the agreement of the leaders in Congress. The outrage following the Saturday Night Massacre led to voicing what had been unthinkable till then: Nixon should be impeached. (The resignation of Vice-President Spiro Agnew on unrelated tax evasion charges in October increased opponents' willingness to see the president replaced by the less controversial new vice-president, Gerald Ford.) By February 1974 the House of Representatives asked the Judiciary Committee to begin impeachment hearings. In March, after reviewing the tapes that the president finally released (two of the nine were missing, and the tape recording of the first conversation after the break-in contained a suspicious gap of 18 minutes), a federal grand jury indicted seven persons and secretly named Richard M. Nixon an unindicted co-conspirator. The grand jury gave its information to the House Judiciary Committee.

Both the Judiciary Committee and the special prosecutor's office requested an additional sixty-four tapes from the president. In April Jaworski asked Judge Sirica to order Nixon to turn over the tapes. Once again claiming executive privilege, Nixon refused. In late May Sirica ordered the president to give him the tapes for his examination. The president appealed. On May 24, 1974, Jaworski dramatized the importance of the case by taking an unusual step. He bypassed the U.S. Court of Appeals and asked the Supreme Court to grant *certiorari*—an order to the lower court to send the case to the higher court for review. And so, almost two years after the ill-fated bugging of Democratic headquarters, the U.S. Supreme Court took the case of *United States v. Nixon*.[8]

The Issues Before the Court

The political setting involved a president who had undermined his popularity by condoning illegal acts and who many feared was expanding executive power into an "imperial presidency."[9] There were two overlapping legal issues before the Court: separation of powers and its impact on the president's claim of executive privilege.

The president's lawyer argued that judicial review did not apply, questioning whether the Court had the authority to judge the president's actions in this dispute. He based his case on a strict interpretation of the constitutional doctrine of separation of powers. Separation of powers meant a claim to "absolute executive privilege against inquiry by the coordinate Judicial Branch." This interpretation made the president's conversations with White House aides confidential, and only he could decide whether tapes of them should be released. Nixon's clash with the special prosecutor was a dispute *within* the executive branch between the president and a subordinate, which the chief executive had the sole authority to resolve. The president's lawyer suggested that the Court's decision would be advisory, not binding. In short, the Supreme Court could not use judicial review to reverse the president's actions. This challenge to the Court's institutional power would ultimately motivate a unified response from the justices.[10]

For the special prosecutor, the president's claim to executive privilege had no constitutional basis. Even if there was a privilege for executives to withhold information, the idea that the president had non-reviewable power to determine what information would be released had never been established. The federal courts retained the power to review presidential actions involving the special prosecutor. The separation of powers had never been an absolute bar against judicial review, *unless* the courts themselves decided that an issue was outside their jurisdiction. To remove any president from judicial authority was troubling. In his oral argument, Jaworski got to the heart of the matter:

> Now enmeshed in almost 500 pages of briefs, when boiled down, this case really presents one fundamental issue. Who is to be the arbiter of what the Constitution says? . . . In his public statements, as we all know, the President has embraced the Constitution as offering him support for his refusal to supply the subpoenaed tapes. Now the President may be right in how he reads the Constitution, but he may also be wrong. And if he is wrong, who is there to tell him so? And if there is no one, then the President, of course, is free to pursue his course of erroneous interpretations. What then becomes of our constitutional form of government?[11]

Jaworski shaped his argument as if a person named Nixon had important evidence that was needed for a criminal case. He made the stunning point that the president was only using executive privilege in this case to conceal a criminal conspiracy, not the legitimate business of his office. But the prosecutor still had to contend with the president's absolutist claim that the right of executive privilege, protected by the separation of powers, prevented any interference by the courts in the president's refusal to turn over the tapes. These tapes would, the president contended, eventually be made available for impeachment proceedings, thus drawing the Court into a political dispute between the two branches. The Court had to determine whether they could judge this case, whether the president had a right of executive privilege, and whether that right extended to protecting the confidentiality of his conversations. These legal issues, while important, were secondary to the extraordinary political crisis surrounding the case.

The Burger Court Waits for the Case

A hard-to-miss aspect of *United States v. Nixon* was that one of the parties had appointed four of the nine justices to the Supreme Court. President Nixon had not only elevated Warren Burger to be chief justice, he also appointed Harry A. Blackmun, who like Burger was from Minneapolis (and remained so close to his friend that they were labeled the "Minnesota Twins"); Lewis F. Powell, a prominent lawyer from Virginia; and William H. Rehnquist, the Burger Court's most conservative jurist and later to be chief justice. These appointments were made with an eye to undermining the liberal decisions of the influential reign of Earl Warren, chief justice from 1953 to 1969. In the end the Burger Court (1969–1986) didn't achieve this, leading a scholar to conclude, "No important Warren Court decision was overturned by the Burger Court."[12]

Part of the reason for the lack of a clear direction from the Court was the holdovers that remained on the bench from the Warren Court. Three of them made up the liberal bloc—Justice William Brennan, who was the chief justice's main adversary; William O. Douglas, a maverick and the Court's senior member; and Justice Thurgood Marshall, the first African American justice. The two remaining justices, Potter Stewart and Byron White, were more conservative, but their independent judicial philosophies made them difficult votes to count on. Also questionable was Burger's leadership. Nixon appointed him for his strong law-and-order positions and, perhaps, because he looked like a Hollywood version of a chief justice with snow-white hair and impressive shoulders. He had been active in the Republican party and served on the court of appeals in Washington, DC. On the bench, he could be aloof and pedantic, focusing on minor details rather than the critical issues at stake. Many of the justices simply didn't respect Burger's intellectual grasp of the law.

This interplay among the justices would be an important ingredient in the case they now faced. *U.S. v. Nixon* was to be, as much as any case in history, a negotiated institutional decision to resolve a major constitutional crisis. It was

The Supreme Court in 1972: Seated in the front row, from left, are Associate Justices Potter Stewart and William O. Douglas, Chief Justice Warren E. Burger, Associate Justices William J. Brennan Jr. and Byron R. White. Standing in the back row, from left, are Associate Justices Lewis F. Powell Jr., Thurgood Marshall, Harry A. Blackmun, and William H. Rehnquist.
AP–Wide World Photos

to be unanimous not because of any shared views of the law among the justices, or even much agreement among themselves on the decision they signed. This exceptional decision was reached as a collective compromise because the justices felt that the stakes of the case, for the government and the Court, were too high to allow dissent. They spoke in one voice because their institution was being challenged. Their decision represented "the rule-of-law defended against attack."[13]

The Law and Politics of a Unanimous Decision

The first issue for the Court was whether to accept the case. When President Nixon refused to deliver the tapes to Judge Sirica in the District Court, Jaworski bypassed the Court of Appeals and went directly to the Supreme Court. While he argued that the case should be expedited because of the important constitutional issues at stake, the understood reason was that Watergate had already paralyzed the government for months. In addition, the impeachment proceedings were starting and to wait for the expected year it would take for the Court to resolve the tapes issue was unthinkable. On May 31, 1974, the Court approved this rare procedure and announced it would hear the case. Justice Rehnquist disqualified himself, because he had served in Nixon's Justice Department with several of the defendants who were now on trial.

In discussing the case in conference, the justices quickly agreed on the major points. They concurred that the Court had jurisdiction and that the case should be decided as soon as possible. They further agreed that Nixon's claim of an absolute executive privilege could not stand, but they disagreed on how much deference they owed to this executive claim. These differences among the justices would be reconciled during the writing of the opinion. Justice Brennan suggested a joint decision, written by all the justices. This unusual option was quickly turned down by the other justices, and Burger asserted the traditional right of the chief justice to write the opinion when he was in the majority. What resulted, however, in the weeks after the conference was an unusually collective drafting process, where the weakness of the Court's leadership and its divisions melded together in a rare institutional decision. The importance of a public show of unanimity by the Court spurred cooperation among the justices.[14]

Burger's first draft caused unhappiness on the bench. Potter Stewart told his clerks that the Chief's paper would have gotten a grade of D in law school and was raised to a B by the efforts of the other justices.[15] The result was what Justice Blackmun called "a palace revolution," with justices taking over different sections of the opinion.[16] Blackmun worked on the statement of facts; the issue of the Court's jurisdiction reflected Douglas's writing; and Powell, Stewart, and Brennan all had a hand in the final section on the president's claims to executive privilege. The irony of having the chief justice accept their revisions and deliver the Court's ruling against the president who had appointed him did not go unnoticed among the justices. The back and forth of various drafts and Burger's accommodations to his justices' objections made the final opinion something less than a legal masterpiece.

Executive privilege produced the most substantive conflict. Although all the justices agreed that Nixon's absolute claim couldn't stand, the questions of whether the Constitution allowed executive privilege and how far it went provoked disagreement. In his early draft, Burger had recognized this right when the president was conducting what the chief justice called "core functions," such as war powers. He added that in the Nixon case this did not apply because the president's claim did not relate to an essential function. Several justices thought that introducing language about core functions implied that the president did have an absolute constitutional authority (which implied no judicial review) over some of his duties, and invited "future chaos." These justices, led by Stewart, wanted a clear assertion of judicial review, worried that Burger was too deferential to presidential power and that this language could give the president wiggle room for not obeying the present case. Burger eventually dropped his core functions language.

The final decision delivered by the Court did find a constitutional basis for executive privilege. For the president to effectively exercise his powers, the Court found that his claim of executive privilege was "rooted in the separation of powers under the Constitution." However, in the present case there was little to back up the president's claim, and when weighed against the prosecutor's need for the information in a pending criminal trial, it wouldn't stand. So in the process of rejecting a specific claim to executive privilege and demanding that the president turn over the tapes, the Court did establish a general constitutional right that a president's communications should be treated as confidential. The Court established this right for the first time with little backing from the historical record.[17]

Conclusion

The dramatic July 24 announcement forcing the president to deliver the tapes came just hours before the House Judiciary Committee began its televised debate on articles of impeachment. It was a devastating moment for the president. Nixon had counted on there being some exception in the decision for national security matters and at least one dissenting justice. He had hoped there would be some "air" in the Court's ruling. He was told by his chief of staff that it was unanimous, with no air in it at all.

"None at all?" Nixon asked.

"It's tight as a drum."

Nixon decided he had no choice but to comply. The wrenching public confrontation between the president and the other branches of government was near an end. Seventeen days later, clearly implicated in the Watergate cover-up by the tapes and facing almost certain impeachment, Nixon became the first president in history to resign.[18]

Columbia Law professor Alan F. Westin wrote that *U.S. v. Nixon* was "one of the most predictable rulings in the history of American constitutional law. The political situation was not only hospitable to a ruling against the President but almost irresistibly pressing for it."[19] The Court resolved the government impasse. It restrained a president who was far out of line with the traditions and practices of his office, and put itself behind his removal. The justices accepted their role and fulfilled their duty to end the Watergate crisis.

But the price of the Court's unanimous agreement was to confirm a broad constitutional right of executive privilege. Although not approving of the president's assertion that he alone could determine the application of executive

President Richard Nixon says an emotional farewell on his resignation from office. His wife, Pat, and daughter, Tricia, look equally unhappy.
© Bettmann/Corbis

privilege, insulated from judicial review, the Court did defer to a vaguely defined privilege, which many considered a strengthening of the presidency. As of now, the judicial precedent has not been widely applied nor has it led to other crises over executive power. Putting legal scholarship to the side, the process of reaching a unanimous decision in *U.S. v. Nixon* underlined that the Supreme Court contained justices with both Washington experience and political savvy.

Notes

1. U.S. Congress. Senate. *Select Committee on Presidential Campaign Activities,* Vol. I (Washington, DC: A Dell Book, 1974).
2. Frank Mankiewicz, *U.S. v. Richard M. Nixon* (New York: Quadrangle, 1975), 13.
3. See Douglas Muzzio, *Watergate Games* (New York: New York University Press, 1982), 15.
4. C-SPAN has excerpts from the Nixon tapes online at: *www.c-span.org/executive/presidential/nixon.asp.*

5. Bob Woodward and Carl Bernstein, *All the President's Men* (New York: Warner Books, 1975).

6. *Select Committee on Presidential Campaign Activities,* 1974, xiii. This is the Ervin Committee's detailed account of the cover-up and related illegal activities by the Nixon White House.

7. A good account of the legal processes can be found in Howard Ball, *"We Have a Duty": The Supreme Court and the Watergate Tapes Litigation* (New York: Greenwood Press, 1990).

8. See Ball, Chapter 2, "The Watergate Scandal Unfolds," 21–38.

9. See Arthur M. Schlesinger Jr., *The Imperial Presidency* (New York: Popular Library, 1973).

10. See Raoul Berger, *Executive Privilege: A Constitutional Myth* (New York: New American Library, 1974), 254–255. Also see Bob Woodward and Scott Armstrong, *The Brethren: Inside the Supreme Court* (New York: Avon Books, 1979), 363.

11. Alan Westin and Leon Friedman, *United States v. Nixon* (New York: Chelsea House Publishers, 1974), 528–529.

12. Bernard Schwartz, *A History of the Supreme Court* (New York: Oxford University Press, 1993), 314.

13. Westin and Friedman, xvi.

14. David M. O'Brien, *Storm Center: The Supreme Court in American Politics,* 3rd ed. (New York: W. W. Norton, 1993), 280–285.

15. Ball, 136.

16. *Washington Post,* March 5, 2004, A12. Excerpts from Blackmun's recently published papers.

17. Ball, 144–146.

18. From Woodward and Armstrong, 412. The most complete coverage of the internal discussions in the Court on *U.S. v. Nixon* can be found here, 337–412.

19. As quoted by Ball, 150.